Dictionary of International Accounting Terms

Series Editor: John O E Clark

Financial World Publishing
IFS House
4-9 Burgate Lane
Canterbury
Kent
CT1 2XJ
United Kingdom

T 01227 818687
F 01227 479641
E editorial@ifslearning.com
W www.ifslearning.com

Financial World Publishing publications are published by The Chartered Institute of Bankers, a non-profit making registered educational charity.

Typeset by Kevin O'Connor

Printed in Spain

ISBN 0-85297-575-9

FINANCIAL WORLD Publishing
THE CHARTERED INSTITUTE OF BANKERS

Preface

This book is intended to provide access to the terms of trade finance for students and professionals in the growing world of internatonal trade, and its interaction with banking and the stock exchange. It should also assist private investors and people who read financial journals and the financial pages of daily newspapers. Like its companion volume, the *Dictionary of International Business Terms*, it does not limit itself merely to well-established terms. It also includes definitions of the everyday jargon, acronyms and newly adopted words (many from the United States) that are now common in national and international financial dealings.

The Dictionary of International Accounting Terms is one of a series of publications complied from The CIB's unique database of dictionary definitions that relate to various aspects of finance and their applications. As a result, some definitions appear in more than one book – as they should to maintain a comprehensive coverage of the subject within a single self-contained volume. The dictionaries in the series published to date include:

Dictionary of International Accounting Terms
0-85297-575-9
Dictionary of International Banking and Finance Terms
0-85297-632-1
Dictionary of International Business Terms
0-85297-574-0
Dictionary of International Insurance and Finance Terms
0-85297-631-3
Dictionary of International Investment and Finance Terms
0-85297-577-5
Dictionary of International Trade Finance
0-85297-576-7

John O E Clark

John O E Clark is a writer and editor who regularly contributes to dictionaries, encyclopedias and other types of information books for publication in Britain and abroad. He specializes in explaining technical subjects to students and other non-experts, and to people whose first language is not necessarily English.

A

AAA Abbreviation of ***American Accounting Association***.

AAPA Abbreviation of ***Association of Authorized Public Accountants***.

AAT Abbreviation of ***Association of Accounting Technicians***.

abatement Reduction. The term is used in the USA to describe the cancellation, in whole or in part, of a government levy.

ABB Abbreviation of ***activity-based budgeting***.

abbreviated accounts Short form of accounts that, under the UK Companies Act 1989, may be filed with the Register of Companies by a small or medium-sized company. They were formerly known as modified accounts.

ABC Abbreviation of ***activity-based costing***.

ability-to-pay taxation Theory of taxation whereby those who are able to pay more are taxed at a higher rate. Ability-to-pay taxation may be applied to luxury goods, which therefore attract a high rate of tax.

abnormal loss Also known variously as abnormal shrinkage, spoilage or waste, the loss (shrinkage, spoilage or waste) that exceeds that expected in a manufacturing or chemical process. Its existence denotes a lack of operating efficiency.

aboriginal cost In the accounting of public utilities in the USA, the ***acquisition cost*** of an asset which is met by the first person or organization using it.

above-the-line Describing items that are included in the ***profit and loss account*** of a business (as distinct from the ***appropriation account***).

above-the-line expenditure *See* ***current expenditure***.

abridged accounts Also called non-statutory accounts, financial statements that are less complete that a company's full report and accounts. It is a requirement of the UK Companies Act 1989 that their abridged form is so stated on the accounts.

absolute bill of sale *See* ***bill of sale***.

absorbed overhead When ***absorption costing*** is being used, the part of a company's overhead that is charged to production. Also called applied overhead or recovered overhead, it equals the product of actual production and the ***absorption rate***.

absorption Use of ***absorption rates*** to allocate a company's overhead to its production. It is a method used in ***absorption costing***.

absorption account In double-entry cost accounting, an account opened to indicate the amount of overhead that has been allocated to production.

absorption costing Method of costing a product that assigns a fixed ***manufacturing overhead*** as well as material and labour costs as a product cost to the units being produced.

absorption rate In a ***absorption costing***, the rate determined before an accounting period so that overheads can be charged to a company's production. It is equal to the budgeted overhead divided by the budgeted production.

abusive tax shelter Type of limited partnership in the USA that, according to the Internal Revenue Service, claims illegal deductions of tax, usually by inflating the real value of property that has been purchased.

Accelerated Cost Recovery System (ACRS) In the USA, an Internal Revenue Service system that permits an arbitrary recovery period to be employed in calculating deductions for depreciation, rather than an item's useful life. By allowing quicker recovery of the cost of an asset it encourages capital investment.

accelerated depreciation Practice of depreciating an asset at a rate greater than the actual decline in its value in order to obtain tax concessions. It need not occur throughout the life of an asset; a substantial proportion of its total value is often written off in the first year, and reduced allowances for depreciation are made thereafter.

acceleration Increase in the rate of a price trend or, if a borrower defaults on a deal, the action of the lender when demanding early repayment.

acceptance Written promise to pay. It is thus equivalent to a ***promissory note.***

acceptance commission Commission charged by a bank for providing ***acceptance credit.***

acceptance credit Way of financing a sale to a foreign buyer in which a commercial or merchant bank provides credit to the foreign creditworthy importer, who can draw a bill of exchange against the credit. The bank charges an ***acceptance commission.***

account (a/c, acc or **acct.)** In general terms, any note kept of a financial transaction, often also referred to as *accounts*. There are two more specific meanings:

1. In banking, it designates an arrangement made to deposit money with a bank, building society or other financial institution. There are various types of such accounts, with different conditions of withdrawal, rates of interest, minimum deposits, and so on, such as current accounts, deposit accounts and savings accounts.
2. On the London Stock Exchange, it is a period of two weeks (usually extended to three weeks when bank holidays occur) in which trading is carried out. Broadly, transactions are made in the two weeks of the account and the relevant paperwork is carried out during the following week, followed by payments (settlements) made on the sixth business day after the end of the account. This method of working allows transactions to be made with deferred payment, enabling speculation to take place.

accountability Requirement to give an account when requested. For example, a company's directors are accountable to its shareholders (which is why they publish an annual report and accounts, as required by the Companies Act).

accountancy Body of knowledge relating to financial matters. It also describes the work done by an ***accountant***, involving a knowledge of the law as it affects financial matters (for example, the tax laws), ***book-keeping*** and the preparation of ***annual accounts***.

It also described the work done by an accountant.

accountant Any person practising ***accountancy***, whether qualified or not. The term may be prefixed by various others, that denote the specialism of the accountant (such as ***cost accountant, management accountant***), that accountant's position within a company (such as chief accountant), or his or her professional qualifications (such as ***certified accountant, Certified Public Accountant, Chartered Accountant***).

Accountant's Index Quarterly bibliography, published by the American Institute of Certified Public Accountants, which lists all of their accounting books and articles.

accountant's lien Legal right to keep goods or property until their owner pays debts due to the person who keeps them.

accountant's opinion Another term for ***auditor's opinion*** in the USA.

accountant's report Another term for ***auditor's report*** in the USA.

account code Code number from a ***chart of accounts*** assigned to a given account. Each feature of the account, such as location, responsible department and type of asset is represented by a number in the code. It is also known as an accounting code, cost code, expenditure code or income code.

account form Type of balance sheet that lists assets on the left-hand side and equities on the right-hand side.

accounting Very broadly, the activity of recording and verifying all monies borrowed, owed, paid or received.

accounting bases Methods employed to apply ***accounting concepts*** to financial statements. A company's particular accounting bases constitute its accounting policy

accounting code Another name for ***account code.***

accounting concepts Also called accounting conventions, accounting methods and accounting principles, the basic concepts by which sets of accounts are made up. The four generally accepted principles are the ***accruals concept, consistency concept, going concern concept*** and ***prudence concept.***

accounting cushion The US practice of making a larger provision for expenses in a particular year, so that they can be minimized in future years. In other words, earnings are initially understated, and then overstated later.

accounting cycle Whole sequence of procedures in accounting that begin with ***journal entries*** in the books of account and end with the ***post-closing trial balance*** or ***financial statements***.

accounting entity Organization for which accounting records are kept, such as a company, corporation, partnership or sole trader. It may or not be the same as the corresponding legal entity. For example, a sole trader is an accounting entity but he or she may not be the outright owner of the business and therefore not the legal entity.

accounting equation Put simply, it is:

assets = liabilities + capital (owner's equity)

and it underlies all ***balance sheets***. In order for the balance sheet to balance, any decrease or increase in total assets must be matched by a corresponding increase or decrease in the liabilities and capital.

accounting errors Corrections in the accounts for the current period that identify arithmetic errors or incorrect application of accounting principles in the previous accounts. They are usually dealt with as debits or credits to ***retained earnings***.

accounting event Anything recorded, as a debit or credit, in accounting records as a transaction.

accounting exposure Risk arising from the translation of assets and liabilities into foreign currency. It is also known as translation exposure.

accounting manual Document detailing the accounting policies of a company, usually including a ***chart of accounts*** or ***account codes***.

accounting for inflation Most published accounts employ the principles of ***historic cost accounting***. But in an inflationary period, they do not give an accurate picture of present real value of capital employed or real profits. The usual way of overcoming this difficulty is by the adoption of ***current cost accounting***.

accounting methods An alternative term for ***accounting concepts***.

accounting period Time for which accounts are prepared, such as a year for a company's financial accounts or a month for internal management accounts.

accounting plan Detailed guide to accounting issued by France, Spain and various other European countries. It includes such items as a chart of accounts as well as definitions of accounting terms and rules. Accountants are expected to use the plan in the preparation of financial statements.

accounting policies Another term for ***accounting bases***, particularly as adopted by a particular ***accounting entity***.

accounting principles Alternative term for ***accounting concepts***.

Accounting Principles Board (APB) The forerunner in the USA of the ***Financial Accounting Standards Board*** (FASB). It operated from 1959 to 1973, during which time it acted as a private regulatory body, setting accounting concepts for use in the USA through the publication of 31 *APB Opinions*.

accounting procedures Methods needed to put ***accounting concepts*** into practice, sometimes taken to mean the concepts themselves.

accounting profit Profit found by using accepted accounting concepts, i.e. revenue less expenses, without the application of taxation regulations. It may present the financial status of a company in a better light than if proper ***accounting standards*** are applied.

accounting rate of return Ratio of income divided by average investment for a given period. Because it is not based on discounted cash flows (but merely gross income), neglecting taxation or interest, it can give an unrealistic picture of the situation, hence its alternative name unadjusted rate of return.

accounting ratio One of several ratios considered important in assessing the financial viability of a company. They include the ***current ratio*** and the ***liquid ratio***.

accounting records In compliance with the Companies Act 1985, every company has to keep records of its accounts, which give an accurate picture of its trading activities. The records may and notified to Companies House. They may be manual (in ledgers, journals, etc., supported by invoices and other documentation) or stored on a computer.

accounting reference date End date of an ***accounting reference period***, usually the last day of the month that is the anniversary of the company's incorporation.

accounting reference period Company's ***financial year***, as defined in its ***articles of association*** and notified to Companies House.

accounting standards Standards by which a company's ***annual accounts*** are drawn up. They are set by professional bodies such as the ***Accounting Standards Board*** (ASB) in the UK or the ***Accounting Principles Board*** (APB) in the USA (where they are usually known as accounting principles or concepts).

Accounting Standards Board (ASB) Organization established in the UK in 1990 (when it replaced the ***Accounting Standards Committee***) to set up and improve standards in the world of accountancy.

Accounting Standards Committee (ASC) Organization established in the UK in 1976 which issued various ***Statements of Standard Accounting Practice (SSAPs)***. In 1990 it was superseded by the ***Accounting Standards Board.***

accounting system Any method of recording and evaluating a company's accounting transactions.

accounts An alternative term for a company's ***books of accounts*** or the ***profit and loss account*** together with the ***balance sheet***.

accounts, nominal, real and personal Three broad categories of accounts sometimes employed in book-keeping. Nominal accounts deal with revenue and expenditure, real accounts give details of assets and capital, and personal accounts list all creditors and debtors.

accounts payable Accounts on which a company owes money and for which it has been invoiced. They are also sometimes referred to as trade creditors and are a ***current liability*** on the balance sheet.

accounts receivable Accounts on which money is owed to a company and for which it has issued invoices. They are also sometimes referred to as trade debtors and are a ***current asset*** on the balance sheet.

accounts receivable turnover Ratio of net sales for a period and the average balance of net accounts receivable.

account stated Legally binding account that shows an agreed balance between two parties, one of whom owes the other.

accretion Increase in the value of an asset because of physical (usually natural) change, such as the growth of trees in a plantation.

accrual Gradual increase in something by addition over a period of time (and not resulting from a specific transaction). *See also* ***accrued charge***.

accrual accounting Method of accounting in which revenue is entered when it is earned (but not yet necessarily received) and expenses are recognized when they are incurred (but not necessarily paid for). It thus differs fundamentally from ***cash-flow accounting***.

accrual basis Another term for the method employed in ***accrual accounting***.

accruals concept One of the basic ***accounting concepts*** by which income and expenditure are taken into the profit and loss account for the period in which they are earned or occur. It is useful in that it pulls together receipts and the costs incurred in generating them, avoiding the lag between the time income is received and the time liabilities become due.

accrue To accumulate during a specific period even though no specific transaction occurs.

accrued Describing income or expenditure that has been earned or occurred although not yet received or paid. *See* ***accruals concept***.

accrued charge Also called accrued liability, a charge that has not been accounted for or paid. For example, demand for rent made in arrears must appear on the accounts as an accrued charge, because the service had already been used but not paid for. *See* ***accrual***.

accrued depreciation Alternative term for ***accumulated depreciation***.

accrued expense Another name for ***accrued charge***.

accrued income Also called accrued revenue, income that has been earned but not yet received (within a given accounting period). It is treated as a current asset on the balance sheet. See ***accruals concept***.

accrued interest Interest payment that is due, but not yet received.

accrued liability Another name for ***accrued charge***.

accrued payable Payable, such as interest or salaries, that results from the passage of time.

accrued receivable Receivable, such as revenue from rents, that results from the passage of time.

accumulated depreciation Total value of an asset that has been written off so far. It is also known as accrued depreciation, aggregate depreciation and allowance for depreciation.

accumulated earnings Another term for ***accumulated profits***.

accumulated fund Fund held by a club or other non-profit making organization which is built up from surplus income (or from which a deficit may be funded). It is thus equivalent to the capital of a profit-making organization, and for this reason is sometimes known as a capital fund.

accumulated profits Also called accumulated earnings, the amount shown in the appropriation account that can be carried forward (after allowing for reserves and paying items such as dividends and taxes).

accurate presentation Requirement that financial statements should match as accurately as possible the economic effects of transactions.

acid-test ratio Ratio of a company's assets (excluding stock) to its current liabilities. It is also called the liquid or liquidity ratio or the quick ratio (because it gives a quick assessment of a company's financial state).

ACMA Abbreviation of Associate of the ***Chartered Institute of Management Accountants***.

acquisition accounting Procedures introduced after a company has been taken over. The acquired company's results, including tangible and intangible assets (excluding goodwill) are taken into the consolidated profit and loss account only from the date of the take-over.

acquisition cost Net invoice price of an asset plus costs incurred in acquiring it and making it ready for use (such as legal fees, freight and installation costs).

ACRS Abbreviation of ***Accelerated Cost Recovery System***.

ACT Abbreviation of ***advance corporation tax*** and ***Association of Corporate Treasurers***.

acting in concert Action of a number of people working together in an organization's affairs, either by formal or informal agreement.

activity Any cost-incurring operation within an organization, which probably includes practically everything that happens.

activity accounting Another term for ***responsibility accounting***.

activity-based budgeting (ABB) Assigning resource to activities within a budget by identifying those activities and how they interact and incur cost.

activity-based costing (ABC) Alternative to ***absorption costing*** which acknowledges that every ***activity*** within an organization incurs cost and therefore the products or users of that activity should bear its cost.

activity-based depreciation Method of calculating the depreciable life of an asset in terms of units of output it produces or in units of time it is actually in use.

activity costing Another term for ***activity-based costing***.

activity ratio In any accounting period, the production actually achieved divided by the best level of production that is theoretically possible.

actual costing Costing of an organization's activities based on the real costs of materials, labour and overhead.

actuarial Describing analyses or calculations that involve compound interest and probabilities.

addback method Way of setting out a statement of financial position changes by beginning with the net income and then adding back (or deducting) any items that do not affect the working capital.

added-value statement Financial statement that shows, for a given period, how much value has been added by the collective contributions of a company's capital and labour force. It is equal to the turnover less the cost of materials and bought-in items. It is also known as a value-added statement.

additional paid-in capital Account that itemizes the amount received by the issuer of capital stock over and above its stated (par) value. It is also termed capital contributed in excess of stated (par) value.

adjudication For a given document, the Inland Revenue's assessment of the amount of stamp duty due on it. The term is also used to describe the decision of a court, as in a bankruptcy case.

adjunct account Account in which additions to another account are itemized. The overall liability at any given time is the sum of the two account balances.

adjustable-rate mortgage (ARM) Mortgage in which the rate of interest varies throughout the term (often to keep pace with the base lending rate).

adjusted acquisition cost Cost of an asset adjusted for subsequent changes in price levels.

adjusted bank balance of cash Balance on a company's bank statement adjusted (up or down) for such items as outstanding cheques not presented to the bank or unrecorded deposits, thus reconciling the bank statement with the current actual cash balance.

adjusted book balance of cash Balance in a company's account for cash in the bank adjusted (up or down) for such items as bank charges, thus reconciling the account balance with the actual cash held.

adjusted gross income In the USA, the difference between a taxpayer's gross income and the adjustments to his or her income.

adjusted trial balance Trial balance of an account adjusted for such items as recent accruals and prepayments, before closing entries are included; debits and credits are listed separately. It is then used to draw up the profit and loss account for the balance sheet.

adjusting entry Entry that updates an account, usually added at the end of the accounting period to allow for a transaction that was improperly recorded or omitted previously (such as late adjustments for accruals, depreciation and prepayments).

adjusting event Also known as a post-balance-sheet event, an event that occurs after the date of the balance sheet but before the final accounts are approved (such as depreciation in some of the company's assets).

adjusting journal entry (AJE) Journal entry that records something which must be posted to a ***ledger account***. An example would be a prepayment that occurred at the end of the accounting period.

adjustment Change to an account caused by an ***adjusting entry***.

administration cost variance Difference between the actual administration overheads incurred during an accounting period and those that were budgeted.

administration expense General expense that includes all those incurred in the overall management of a company, but not positively attributable to any particular department or operating arm.

administration order County Court order requiring the administration of the estate of a debtor, who usually has to pay the debts by instalments in order to avoid bankruptcy.

administration overheads Part of a company's general overheads that are attributable to its administrative activities, such as the cost of general office staff and their equipment, company stationery, and so on.

administrative receiver Person who is appointed by the court to manage a company's assets on behalf of debenture holders and other secured creditors.

administrator Person who is appointed (usually by the court) to manage somebody else's property, or a person who is appointed by the court to manage the affairs of somebody who has died intestate (without making a will). Proof of his or her authority is a letter of administration issued by the court.

ADR Abbreviation of ***asset depreciation range***.

advance Part-payment for goods or services made ahead of total payment and before the goods or services are made available. If payment depends on sales, the advance may be set against the receipts from those sales.

advance corporation tax (ACT) In the UK, corporation tax is levied in two parts. The first part is levied on the distribution of profits and is known as advance corporation tax. The second half of the tax is estimated on the company's earnings. *See also* ***corporation tax***.

advancement Pre-payment by a living parent to a child of an amount that the child would receive as a beneficiary after the death of the parent.

advance payment bond Company's guarantee (usually through its bankers) that any advance payment will be refunded to a customer if the company cannot deliver the goods or services contracted for.

advance to an affiliate Loan made to a subsidiary by its parent company, on whose balance sheet it is shown as a noncurrent asset.

adverse balance In general, an account balance that shows a loss or liability. The term is also short for adverse balance of trade.

adverse opinion Auditor's report that states that a company's financial statements are not fair or do not comply with generally accepted accounting principles.

adverse variance Difference between budgeted and actual financial performance that leads to a reduction in budgeted profit (usually because of higher costs than expected or less sales revenue than expected).

advice note Note from a supplier giving details of goods ordered or delivered. It may accompany or precede the actual shipment, and precedes the invoice. *See also* ***delivery note***.

affiliated company Company that is associated in some way with another company. Of no legal standing in the UK, the term has confusingly two opposite meanings in the USA. It may be a company that controls another company, or a company that is controlled by another company.

after closing Describing a trial balance at the end of the accounting period, also termed postclosing in the USA.

after cost Describing an expenditure made after a revenue has been received (such as repairs carried out under a warranty agreement). After costs should be acknowledged at the time of the sale and included in estimated liabilities (or estimated expenses).

age analysis Listing of debts in the order of how long they have been outstanding, an important aspect of proper credit control. In the USA, the system is described as an ageing schedule or as ageing accounts receivable.

agency fee Fee paid to a lender's agent for the continuing work involved in managing a loan. It is also termed a facility fee.

agency fund Where a government organization acts as an agent or trustee, an account for holding the assets it receives.

agent Person or company that has entered into a contract of agency with another party and acts as its representative, usually in buying and selling goods and services.

aggregate depreciation An alternative term for ***accumulated depreciation***.

AIAB Abbreviation for Associate of the ***International Association of Bookkeepers***.

AICPA Abbreviation of ***American Institute of Certified Public Accountants***.

AJE Abbreviation of ***adjusting journal entry***.

alienation of assets Sale, by a borrower, of assets that have been used as security to obtain the loan, usually precluded by the loan agreement.

alimony In the USA, payment in a divorce settlement, which is deducted from the payer's gross income for tax purposes. The recipient, however, pays income tax on alimony.

all capital earnings rate Method of gauging a company's operating performance obtained by dividing net income plus interest by average total assets.

all financial resources All of a company's assets minus its liabilities. It is used in the USA to compile a statement of changes in financial position.

all-inclusive income concept Method of compiling a profit and loss account that establishes earning by taking into account all items of profit and loss. Sales of assets and other one-off items may result in a misleading picture.

allocation Assignment of revenue or cost to one or more parts of an organization according to some measure of contribution or benefit.

allowable capital loss Amount by which the sum received by the disposal of an asset is less than what was paid for it.

allowance On a balance sheet, it is a contra account entry in regard to depreciable assets and receivables. A sales allowance is a reduction in price to compensate a buyer because goods are imperfect or not exactly as ordered. An expense allowance is a sum given to an employee to pay for the cost of travel (in the course of work) and other out-of-pocket expenses.

allowance for depreciation *See* ***accumulated depreciation***.

allowance for doubtful debts For a given accounting period, a provision to cover debts that are probably not going to be paid. It is also termed provision for doubtful debts.

allowance for uncollectables On accounts receivable, a contra entry based on an estimate of accounts that will not be collected. It is equivalent to an allowance (or provision) for bad debts.

all-purpose financial statement US term for financial statements designed to be examined by a wide range of interested parties, known in the UK as a ***general-purpose financial statement***.

alpha risk and beta risk Inadequacies in the sampling procedure used by an auditor. The exclusion of a population that should have been included is an alpha risk; the inclusion of a population that should have been excluded is a beta risk.

alternative accounting rules Variations in the historical-cost convention for valuing assets, allowed under the Companies Act 1985, known as the modified historical cost convention. For example, tangible fixed assets may be assigned market value and intangible assets (excluding goodwill) may be valued at current cost.

alternative budgets As well as the budget adopted by an organization, other budgets produced for management consideration (usually based on alternative policies that are not in the event pursued).

alternative costs Costs that would have to be met if alternative policies or assumptions were adopted.

American Accounting Association (AAA) Organization founded in 1916 as the American Association of University Instructors in Accounting. It adopted its present title 20 years later. As implied by its original name, it is primarily for academic accountants, although membership is open to anyone interested in the profession.

American Institute of Certified Public Accountants (AICPA) Professional organization, founded in 1887, to which practising certified public accountants belong in the USA. It oversees the Uniform CPA Examination, although each state also has its own qualification requirements.

American Society of Women Accountants Professional organization to which practising women accountants belong in the USA.

amortization Spreading the cost of a fixed asset over a period of time, rather than writing the total cost into the profit and loss account when it is first bought. Debt repayment can also be amortized in this way. The term is sometimes used to mean ***depreciation*** in the USA.

A

amortization cost Accumulated depreciation of an asset to date, the part of its value that has been written off.

amortizing loan Loan for which the repayments are made as a series of instalments.

amortization schedule List of dates on which loan repayments are due. *See* ***amortization.***

analysis of variance (ANOVA) Breakdown of the variance in a company's total profit into fractions assigned to various activities or departments. It attempts to determine why actual profit differed from the company's budgeted profit.

analytical auditing Method in auditing to determine whether the picture presented is reasonable, by comparing internal and external financial and non-financial data.

analytical review Test in auditing to determine the accuracy and completeness of financial accounts and financial statements. It employs comparisons and statistical methods applied to financial and non-financial data.

annual accounts Report, submitted each year, showing the current financial state of a company and the results of its operations for that year. *See also* ***annual report.***

annualization Procedure in the USA, required by the Internal Revenue Service, in which monthly taxable income is determined by multiplying taxable income for part of a year by 12 and dividing by the number of months concerned.

annualized percentage rate (APR) Also known as annual percentage rate, the rate of interest charged on a monthly basis (e.g. for credit) shown as a yearly compound rate (*see* ***compound interest***).

annual report Document required under company law to be released every year by public companies, describing the company's activities during the previous year. It usually includes the company's balance sheet for that year. It may be combined with the annual accounts as the annual report and accounts.

annual return In the UK, a document that must be submitted to Companies House each year by every company with share capital, detailing such items as the address of the registered office, a list of current members, charges on the company, and so on.

annual value Income that accrues annually from the possession of, say, property or a portfolio of shares. A distinction is normally made between net annual value and gross annual value, the former being the annual income from a possession after expenses of ownership have been deducted, and the latter being the income before expenses have been taken into account.

annuity method Way of calculating a fixed asset's depreciation as a fairly constant annual charge. In the earlier years, when interest costs are high, a low depreciation charge is made, rising in later years as interest costs fall. *See also* ***declining-balance depreciation***; ***straight-line depreciation***.

ANOVA Abbreviation of ***analysis of variance***.

Anton Piller order Court injunction that permits a person to enter named premises to copy certain specified documents. It is generally used to prevent someone from destroying documentary evidence.

APB Abbreviation of ***Accounting Principles Board*** and ***Auditing Practices Board***.

APC Abbreviation of ***Auditing Practices Committee***.

application controls In computerized accounting, application-specific controls that relate to transactions and standing data, ensuring completeness and that the correct data is used. They may be pre-programmed or applied manually by the operator.

application of funds Any transaction that results in a reduction in funds, such as working capital.

applied cost Cost allocated to an activity, company department or product. It is not necessarily the actual cost incurred.

applied overhead Overhead cost charged to an activity, company department or product. It is a type of ***absorption costing*** and not necessarily the actual overhead involved.

apportionment Allocation of a part of costs to a ***cost centre*** which, although it shares in incurring the costs, is not directly responsible for them.

appraisal Use of an expert's opinion, rather than market factors, to value an asset or liability. The term is also used to describe the process of assessing possible alternative courses of action.

appraisal method of depreciation Way of calculating depreciation by valuing an asset at the beginning and the end of a financial period and subtracting the two figures. The depreciation, if any, is then charged to the profit and loss account as an expense. The practice is not generally accepted in the USA.

appreciation Increase in the value of an asset resulting from a rise in market price (often due to inflation).

appropriation In general, the putting aside of funds for a special purpose. In company accounting, it is the division of pre-tax profits between corporation tax, company reserves and dividends to shareholders (*see also* next entry). In another application, if a debtor makes a payment to a creditor and does not specify which debt the payment is in settlement of, the creditor may appropriate it to any of the debts outstanding on the debtor's account. This latter procedure is often known as appropriation of payments. In the USA, appropriation also describes an authorization to spend up to a certain amount.

appropriation account Account that shows net profits (current and carried forward) and how they are split between dividends and reserves. In the USA, it may be an account set aside to accommodate funds that have been authorized for a particular purpose.

appropriation of payments *See* ***appropriation***.

a priori theories of accounting Theories that use economic theory and reasoning to evaluate and measure accounting systems, rather than practical experience.

archive Store for data that is rarely required. It may take the form of various documents or computer storage media such as magnetic tapes or disks. Important computer data may also be held on archive copies in case the original disks are damaged or lost.

Argenti's failure model Technique that allocates scores to such factors as management errors, company defects and symptoms of failure to predict whether or not a company is likely to become bankrupt.

ARM Abbreviation of ***adjustable-rate mortgage***.

arm's length Describing a transaction negotiated and entered into by unrelated parties, each of whom acts in his or her own best interest using fair market values. It is assumed that, unless there is a related party disclosure, all transactions described in financial statements are conducted at arm's length.

arrears Money owed but not yet paid.

articled clerk Type of apprentice, usually working in one of the professions, such as accounting or law.

articulate US term that describes the relationship between an operating statement (explaining a change in an important category on the balance sheet) and comparative balance sheets.

articulated accounts In double-entry book-keeping of profit and loss accounts, an account in which the retained profit is made equal to the increase in the company's net worth as shown on the balance sheet.

ASB Abbreviation of ***Accounting Standards Board***.

ASC Abbreviation of ***Accounting Standards Committee***.

assess To estimate the value of something (as for taxation purposes).

assessed valuation The estimated value of property used by the US government in determining taxes to be paid.

asset Something that belongs to a person or company and which has value, an economic resource (for example buildings, plant, stock and accounts receivable). There are several types of assets for business purposes, and they are usually classified in terms of their availability for exchange. Examples include ***tangible*** and ***intangible assets***, and long-term (US long-lived or noncurrent) and short-term (or current) assets. *See* ***asset classification***.

asset-backed fund Fund consisting of investments that are related to ***tangible assets*** (such as property or shares), so that the investment participates in growth and can be regarded as a hedge against inflation.

asset classification Basic classification is into fixed (held on a continuing basis) and current (held on a short-term basis). Fixed assets may be ***intangible*** or ***tangible***, and they depreciate during their lifetime. Current assets include cash (in hand and at bank), prepayments and stock. It is a legal requirement to classify assets on a company's balance sheet.

asset cover Measure of a company's solvency equal to the ratio of net assets to debt. High asset cover implies that a company is more than marginally solvent.

asset deficiency Company's situation when its assets are less than its liabilities, implying insolvency.

asset depreciation range (ADR) For a particular depreciable asset, the range of depreciable lives permitted by the US Internal Revenue Service.

asset turnover Net sales divided by average assets. It is one of the ratios used in the USA to assess the operations of a company over a given period.

asset revaluation reserve Under ***alternative accounting rules***, the reserve account into which unrealized profit or loss resulting from revaluation of an asset must be included. It is also known as the revaluation reserve account.

assets register List of a company's fixed assets, recording such factors as their cost, estimated economic life, estimated value, location, method of depreciation and revaluation (if any). In manufacturing companies it may be called a plant register.

asset valuation Estimate of the value of a company's assets, to be included on the balance sheet. It may involve a professional ***revaluation***.

asset value Value of a company's assets less its liabilities. It is often divided by the number of issued ordinary shares and expressed as the asset value per share, theoretically payable to shareholders if the company were to be wound up.

assignment Legal transfer of a property, right or obligation from one party to another. Assignment most commonly takes place where a contract is involved. Acknowledging it is also called an assignment, or deed of assignment.

Association of Accounting Technicians (AAT) Organization established in 1980 by the ***Consultative Committee of Accountancy Bodies*** (CCAB). It grants an accounting qualification, which can subsequently be upgraded to a full CCAB qualification.

Association of Authorized Public Accountants (AAPA) Organization whose members are UK-qualified accountants authorized by the Department of Trade to carry out company audits.

Association of Corporate Treasurers (ACT) Organization that promotes the study and practice of company treasury management.

attachment Laying legal claim to the assets of a borrower (or debtor) by the lender (or creditor) because the borrower has failed to make repayments on time.

attainable standard Level of a cost or income standard that is set as being attainable by the people concerned.

attest In auditing, the giving of an opinion that an organization's financial statements are true and fair. It is also called attest function.

attest function *See* ***attest***.

attributable profit For an unfinished long-term contract, the fraction of the total estimated profit attributable to the work that has been completed by a particular date.

audit Examination of a company's accounts. It is a legal requirement in the UK that the accounts of limited companies over a certain size (and certain other organizations) be scrutinized annually by an independent auditor. This is termed a statutory audit, from which small companies (with a turnover of not more than £90,000 and not more than £1.4 million on the balance sheet) are exempt.

Audit Commission for Local Authorities in England and Wales Usually known merely as the Audit Commission, an organization established in 1982 to carry out external audits of the financial accounts of health authorities and local authorities.

audit committee In the USA, a committee on a company's board of directors which chooses the external auditors and discusses the audit with them. In the UK, it is a similar group of non-executive directors which checks auditing functions and financial reporting as put in place by the executive directors.

audit completion checklist List of things to be checked by auditors, usually at the end of an audit, to make sure that accounts being examined give a true and fair view of a company's affairs.

audit evidence All of the information an auditor needs in order to give an opinion of a company's financial statements. Test of internal controls (compliance tests) and an analytical review and tests of details (substantive tests) provide much of such evidence.

audit exemption *See* ***audit***.

audit fee Sum an auditor is paid for carrying out an audit, which has to be approved at the company's annual general meeting (AGM) and itemized in the company accounts. It is sometimes alternatively called auditors' remuneration.

auditing guidelines Guide to the application of auditing standards issued by the ***Auditing Practices Board (APB)***, and formerly by the ***Auditing Practices Committee (APC)***.

Auditing Practices Board (APB) Organization established in 1991, when it replaced the ***Auditing Standards Committee (ASC)***. Half the members come from outside the auditing profession, making it more independent than its predecessor. It is concerned with maintaining high standards of auditing by guiding the development of the profession and its practices.

Auditing Practices Committee (APC) Organization established in 1976 as a committee of the ***Consultative Committee of Accountancy Bodies (CCAB)***. In 1991 it was superseded by the ***Auditing Practices Board (APB)***.

auditing standards Between 1980 and 1991, standards published by the ***Auditing Practices Committee (APC)***. They were then replaced by Statements of Auditing Standards (SAS), issued by the ***Auditing Practices Board (APB)***. Their function is to list essential procedures and reinforce basic principles of auditing. In the USA, a set of ten auditing standards are issued by the Auditing Standards Board of the American Institute of Certified Public Accountants (AICPA).

Auditing Standards Board *See* ***auditing standards***.

audit manual Document detailing a company's auditing policies and procedures.

auditor Person appointed by a company or other organization to carry out an audit. In the UK, in order to act as an external auditor he or she must be registered or a member of a recognized supervisory body.

auditors' remuneration *See* ***audit fee***.

auditors' report Report produced by external auditors appointed to audit a company's accounts, giving an opinion of the financial statements. Under the Companies Act 1985, it has to be filed with the accounts at the Registrar of Companies. In the USA, an auditor's report is sometimes called the accountant's report. *See also* ***auditors' opinion***.

auditors' opinion Opinion contained in an ***auditor's report***. It comments on the way the financial statements have been presented and whether they are adequate. If everything is satisfactory, the auditor gives an unqualified opinion; a qualified opinion is given if there are any doubts.

audit plan Plan, drawn up by an auditor, defining the ***audit strategy*** and procedures that will be applied to each part of a client's accounting system and financial statements.

audit programme Programme of separate audit tests that will be carried out to conform to an ***audit strategy***. It also effectively guarantees the quality control of an audit by recording the work carried out and the various conclusions that are come to.

audit risk Risk that an auditor will fail to qualify his or her audit report even though financial statements may be materially misleading. The presence of misstatements because of a failure of the internal control system to detect them gives rise to control risk; the presence of misstatements undetected by the auditor's ***substantive tests*** results in detection risk; and the absence of proper controls can lead to an inherent risk.

audit rotation Practice of changing auditors every so often (such as five-yearly), to overcome any danger that a company's directors may exercise control of the audit.

audit strategy Overall plan for an audit. For example, it outlines the ***substantive tests*** in terms of their nature, extent and timing.

audit trail System by means of which each stage of a transaction is formally documented and recorded , so that they can be examined during an audit.

authorized auditor Until 1978, a person authorized to be a company's auditor by the Department of Trade or the Secretary of State, under the requirements of the Companies Act 1967. Under the Companies Act 1989, an authorized auditor may act in that capacity only for an unquoted company.

available hours Number of working hours available during an accounting period, or the number available to finish a specific task. They may be expressed as direct labour hours, machine hours or production hours.

average collection period Also called debtor collection period, the average time it takes a company to collect trade debts.

average cost For a unit of output, the total costs (fixed and variable) divided by the number of units produced.

average costing Way of finding a unit cost by dividing the total production cost by the number of units produced.

average cost pricing Determination of a selling price in accordance with the ***average cost*** of producing a good. The manufacturer makes neither a profit nor a loss.

avoidable cost Cost that does not have to be met if an alternative course of action is taken. For example if production of an item ceases, its associated material and labour costs are avoided.

B

BAA Abbreviation of ***British Accounting Association***.

back duty Also known as back tax, retrospective tax levied on profits or goods on which no tax was paid at the time.

backflush accounting Way of avoiding the complications of ***absorption costing*** by keeping minimum levels of stock, so that stock valuation is less important. Profitability is established by apportioning actual costs between cost of sales and stocks held. ***Work in progress*** is not accounted for.

backlog depreciation Depreciation charge that results when an asset is revalued (upwards). Accumulated depreciation also increases.

back-to-back credit Form of credit in which a finance house acts as an intermediary between a foreign seller and a foreign buyer, concealing the identity of the seller. The seller passes to the finance house the documents relevant to the sale and the finance house reissues them to the buyer in its own name.

bad debt Debt that has not been, and is not expected to be, paid. Such losses are practically unavoidable in business (and allowances are almost always made for such instances), although some bad debts may be sold to a factoring company, which attempts to recover the debt on its own account. In company accounts, bad debts are written off to the profit and loss account or to a provision for bad and doubtful debts.

bad debt expense Also called uncollectible accounts adjustment to sales, the contra-revenue account representing loss of income resulting from accounts receivable that cannot be collected.

bad debt recovery Collection (if only partly) of an account receivable that had earlier been written off as uncollectible. The sum is written back to the profit and loss account (or a provision for bad and doubtful debts), or credited to the allowance account or revenue account, depending on the accounting method employed.

bailout period Time that elapses before net accumulated revenue from a project equals or exceeds accumulated outgoings. Potential salvage value of assets is included in the revenue figure.

balance At any specific time, the difference between the total credits and total debits on an account. In double-entry book-keeping, for example, the balance is the sum owed or owing when an account has been reckoned. Hence the phrase to balance the books means to add in this sum to the relevant side of the account so that both columns show the same total.

balance off After totalling the credit and debit sides of an account at the end of an accounting period, to insert a ***balance*** to make them equal.

balance sheet Statement that shows the financial position of a company in respect of its assets and liabilities at a certain time, often the last day of its accounting period, which must be included in the company's financial accounts. It must also give a true and fair view of the company's affairs. After listing the fixed and current assets, and the liabilities (part 1), the statement indicates how they were financed (part 2). The totals of parts 1 and 2 should be equal – they must balance. The balance sheet should also show the corresponding figures for the previous accounting period. In the USA, a balance sheet is sometimes known as a statement of financial condition or position.

balance sheet account Any account that can appear on a company's balance sheet. It is a type of ***permanent account***.

balance-sheet asset value Value of an asset (the book value) as it appears on a company's balance sheet. For a ***tangible asset***, it equals its cost minus any accumulated depreciation. For an ***intangible asset***, it is its cost minus amortization. For ***circulating assets***, it equals the cost or net realizable value, whichever is the lower.

balance-sheet audit Audit whose function is only to confirm the information about assets and liabilities on a company's balance sheet.

balance-sheet equation Simple form of the ***accounting equation***.

balance-sheet format Either of the two ways of presenting a balance sheet as permitted by the Companies Act. It may be vertical or horizontal, with the former containing additionally information about current assets and liabilities. Having chosen one of the formats, a company is expected to stick to it.

balance-sheet total Total net worth of a company as stated at the bottom of its balance sheet (equal to the sum of the fixed assets and current assets minus long-term liabilities).

balancing figure Figure included in order to make two totals equal. *See balance off*.

balloon Large, irregular part-payment during the period of a loan, or (in the USA) a large final repayment of a loan.

bank reconciliation At any time a bank statement is unlikely to agree exactly with the balance in a firm's cash book, because cheques received or paid may not have been banked. A reconciliation is therefore prepared to prove that a true record is being kept by the company. This is done by taking the balance in the cash book, and taking into account transactions not detailed in the statement. At the end of the exercise, the two balances should be the same.

bank reconciliation statement Document issued by a bank to explain any difference between the balance shown on the bank statement and the actual balance as shown by the bank book at a particular time, usually because of a delay in the transmission of credits or presentation of cheques by drawers.

bank report Report from a bank, supplied at the request of an auditor, that itemizes a company's dealings with the bank over a particular period of time.

bankruptcy Condition of a person who is unable to pay his or her debts, as determined by the court (which issues a bankruptcy order). The debts must total at least £750.

bargain purchase Purchase of assets or other property for much less than their market value, usually because the seller is in financial difficulties.

bargain purchase option In the USA, an option that allows a lessee to purchase the leased property for a minimal sum at the end of the lease.

bargain renewal option In the USA, an option that allows a lessee to renew a lease for a nominal rent at the end of the existing lease.

barter Way of obtaining goods or services without using money, by exchanging them for other goods or services. It obviously limits the possibilities of trade, which is why money was introduced and continues to be the principal means of exchange.

base stock method Way of running an inventory that assumes there must always be a minimum or base stock to ensure that an organization's operations can continue. *See also* ***last in first out (LIFO)***. The term is also applied to a method of stock valuation in which stock levels are assumed to be constant and the goods are valued at their original cost.

basic costing method Organization's major method of costing. Possibilities include ***absorption costing, average costing, marginal costing*** and ***process costing***.

basic rate In UK income tax, the rate of tax between the starting rate and the higher rate. In the tax year 2000/2001, it was 23% levied on taxable income between £1501 (up to which the starting rate applied) and £28,000 (over which the higher rate applied). The basic rate was reduced to 22% in April 2000.

basic standard In ***standard costing***, a cost or income standard that is the basis for setting other standards.

basic wage rate Rate of payment to a worker for a certain time period, omitting any extra payments such as shift allowances, overtime or bonuses.

basis Acquisition cost of an asset that is used when calculating gain or loss when it is disposed of or retired from use.

basis of apportionment Sharing of costs equally between several cost centres because overhead cannot be allocated to one specific centre, based on a common factor such as floor area.

basis period Period for which income or profits become the basis for the assessment of tax for that period, usually a year.

basis point Hundredth of a per cent.

basket purchase Purchase of several assets for an all-in price, which then has to be split into several costs (one for each asset) for the purposes of accounting.

batch When units of production are small or identical, a measurement of production (for example, costs are stated 'per batch').

BDV Abbreviation of ***budget-day value***.

batch costing Method of costing in which production is stated in ***batches***, rather than individual units.

bean counters Derogatory and slang term for accountants.

beginning inventory Valuation of stock etc. at the start of an accounting period.

behavioural accounting Type of accounting that, in addition to technical matters, makes allowances for social and psychological aspects.

below-the-line Describing items included in company's profit and loss account that refer to the distribution of profits, such as details of dividends to be paid to shareholders. *See also* ***above-the-line.***

benefit-cost ratio Value of likely benefits from a proposed activity divided by the likely costs. It is a way of evaluating the activity, a ratio of greater than one being favourable.

benefit-in-kind income Benefit that an employee receives instead of or in addition to wages. Examples include company cars, mobile telephones and medical insurance. Most of such benefits can be assigned a value and therefore assessed for income tax.

betterment US term for any improvement, generally one that is capitalized such as the replacement of an old machine with a new one that gives better results.

big bath US slang for the write-off of a significant amount of costs that were previously regarded as assets. It can happen, for example, when a company discontinues an activity in which it invested heavily but which has turned out to be unprofitable.

big GAAP ***Generally accepted accounting principles (GAAP)*** that are used when dealing with large enterprises.

bilateral netting Arrangement whereby two companies set off receipts and payments to each other (usually by single monthly payments), to reduced the bank charges to both organizations.

bill List of charges to be paid on goods or services (also called an invoice and often known as a check in the USA); or a document issued by a bank that promises to pay someone a certain sum of money (usually called a banknote in the UK); or a document describing goods, most often in dealings with customs and excise; or a short term for bill of exchange.

bill of materials Also called a bill of quantities, a specification of the amounts of direct materials that will be needed to achieve a certain output of product.

bill of quantities Another name for ***bill of materials***.

bill of sale Document that certifies the transfer of goods (but not real estate) from one person to another. Goods transferred in this way may not become the property of the receiving person but may be redeemed when the bill is paid, unless they are the subject of an absolute bill of sale.

bills payable Money owed to creditors (such as suppliers to a business). The term is also used for bills of exchange that are held and must be paid at some future date; they are thus effectively liabilities. *See also* ***bills receivable***.

bills receivable Money owed by debtors (such as customers of a business). The term is also used for bills of exchange that are held and due to be paid at some future date; they are thus effectively assets. *See also* ***bills payable***.

bin card Also called a store card, a card at a location (shelf or bin) in a store that details the issuing, receipt and therefore balance of items or quantities of stock.

black economy Illegal economic activity conducted largely for cash by companies and people who pay no taxes on the proceeds.

black market Illegal market that usually deals in scarce or stolen goods. Such markets frequently come into existence in wartime because the goods concerned are rationed or in very short supply, or because the market is exceptionally high – in which case counterfeit or imitation goods often appear. Trading is often in kind, one valued commodity being exchanged for another. *See also* ***grey market***.

blanket rate Fixed charge that relates to a whole series of services or business transactions. It is also an ***absorption rate*** for the production overhead for a whole manufacturing operation.

block grant Lump-sum payment made to a public sector organization, which is at liberty to spend the money as it pleases.

Board of Inland Revenue Group of Inland Revenue Commissioners who administer and collect direct taxes in the UK. These include capital gains tax, corporation tax, income tax, inheritance tax, petrol tax and stamp duties. They operate through tax collectors and tax inspectors.

bona vacantia Describing goods with no obvious owner or claimant, such as the estate of somebody who dies without making a will. Another example is property that remains in the hands of a liquidator after the creditors have been paid. In law it belongs to the Crown.

bonus Additional payment, usually applied to a premium paid in addition to normal salary or wages.

book inventory Inventory that results from consulting records, such as the original inventory plus any subsequent purchases minus invoiced requisitions, rather than by making a physical count.

book-keeper Person employed by a business to keep its books of account, often a member of the ***Association of Accounting Technicians (AAT)***.

book-keeping Practice of keeping records of financial transactions, and analysing them if required. It may be done manually or with the aid of a computer program.

book of original entry Also called book of prime entry, a cash book, day book or journal in which transactions are recorded before being entered into a double-entry book-keeping system.

books In business, the books most frequently referred to are the ***books of account***.

books of account Books in which business transactions are recorded, often consisting of journals, ledgers and various other records of accounts. They are normally held to be legal documents and should indicate the financial position of the business at any time.

book value Also called written-down value, the value shown in a company's books for an asset or liability (or owner's equity), taking due account of any depreciation. Of a company as a whole, it is the amount by which total assets exceed total liabilities (i.e., the net assets).

boot In the USA, an additional sum paid (or received) together with a used item in a trade-in or exchange.

borrowed capital Capital in the form of a loan that is used to finance a business, on which interest has to be paid. It is also called debt capital or loan capital.

bottom line Last line of an account, showing either a profit or a loss. From this sense it has come into general usage to mean the 'brutal truth'.

bought day book US term for a journal in which details of all purchases are recorded, before being transferred to the nominal ledger account.

bought ledger US term for a ledger in which details of sums owed to creditors are recorded.

branch accounting In a business with one or more branches, a method of recording the transactions and financial position of each branch separately, which are therefore regarded as a separate cost centres. The branch accounts are later combined in an overall company statement.

brand value Monetary value assigned to a company's brand name, classified as an intangible asset.

breakeven analysis Management accounting method in which costs are divided into fixed costs and variable costs and then compared with sales revenue. This enables the breakeven point to be established – the level of production, sales volume or sales value that results in neither a profit nor a loss. Managers can then predict the effects of altering any of the parameters (such as sales volume or price). It is also known as cost-volume-profit (CVP) analysis.

breakeven chart Graph on which combined fixed and variable costs are plotted against a range of activity and on which sales revenue is also plotted. The two curves intersect at the ***breakeven point***. *See also* ***breakeven analysis***.

breakeven point Volume of production or sales at which total costs and total revenue are equal. It may be expressed (in terms of units) as fixed costs divided by the contribution per unit, or (in terms of sales) as selling price per unit times fixed costs, divided by contribution per unit. *See also* ***breakeven chart***.

break-up value Of an asset, its value assuming the company holding it will cease trading and that the asset will have to be sold in a hurry (perhaps following a successful take-over of the company).

British Accounting Association (BAA) Organization of accounting academics, formerly called the Association of University Teachers in Accounting.

brought down (b/d) Book-keeping term for an opening balance transferred from the previous record.

brought forward (b/f) Book-keeping term for the total of the corresponding column on the previous page.

budget Plan that details expected future income and outgoings from an activity, normally over the span of a year. It is often referred to in controlling the activity. A budget is also the sum of money set aside for a given activity or project.

budget appropriation Authority to spend (up to a previously a budgeted amount).

budgetary accounts In US government accounting, accounts detailing the estimated costs of various activities.

budgetary control Management of the activities of an organization with reference to an approved budget (so that spending is not allowed to exceed the budgeted amount).

budget committee Unit (usually comprised of managers) whose task is to ensure that an organization's ***budgetary control*** processes are working satisfactorily.

budget cost allowance Amount that a cost centre within an organization is permitted to spend, according to its budget.

budget-day value (BDV) In the UK, value of an asset on Budget Day (6 April) 1995, used to calculate capital gains tax, which was introduced on that day.

budgeted capacity Production capacity, in terms of direct labour hours, machine hours or standard hours, available in a certain period as detailed in the budget for that period.

budgeted cost Expected cost of an activity or unit of production, as expressed in the budget for that item.

budgeted revenue Expected income from an activity or unit of production, as expressed in the budget for that item.

budgeted statements Financial statements drawn up before the relevant activities occur.

budget expenditure head In analysing a budget, one of the principal headings under which financial statements are listed. Usually a particular company manager is responsible for each of the headings.

budget manual Document listing the procedures to be followed in applying *budgetary control*.

budget period Period for which a budget is drawn up (usually a year). Shorter spans within that period may be identified as a means of *budgetary control*.

budget variance Difference between a budget and the actual amount spent.

bullet Final payment of a loan usually consisting of the whole principal (previous payments being of interest only). Or it is a security that pays a guaranteed (fixed) interest at a specific date.

bullet loan Loan in which the whole principal is repaid in the form of a final *bullet*. Interest us usually paid through the previous payments.

burden Alternative US term for *overhead*.

burn rate When a company starts trading using venture capital, the rate at which the company consumes capital in financing fixed overheads. *See venture capital*.

business combination In US accounting practice, the combining into one accounting entity of two or more businesses; a merger.

B

business entity concept Idea that the activities of a business entity, and not of its owners, are the subject of financial accounting and reporting.

business property relief Relief from UK inheritance tax available on business property. The relief is 100% for a business or share in one, and 50% for land or buildings.

business rates In the UK, a local authority tax levied on all businesses.

buy-in Purchase of more than 50% of a company's shares, in order to gain financial and managerial control.

buyout Purchase of a major holding of a company's shares by its existing management.

by-product Secondary product from a process which, although not the main purpose of the operation, is capable of yielding revenue.

C

CA Abbreviation of *Chartered Accountant*.

CAAT Abbreviation of ***computer-assisted auditing technique***.

Cadbury Report Report published in the UK in 1992 by a committee chaired by Sir Adrian Cadbury. The committee was established by the Financial Reporting Council, the Stock Exchange and the accountancy profession. The report recommended that the accounts of a company should contain a statement to the effect that the company's directors had or had not complied with a code of practice regarding the appointment of non-executive directors.

cafeteria plan US term for an arrangement whereby a company employee may chose from among several fringe benefits; that benefit is then not taxable.

Canadian Institute of Chartered Accountants (CICA) Organization established in 1902 (as the Dominion Association of Chartered Accountants) that represents practising accountants in Canada.

cap Upper limit on a charge, such as an interest rate (which could then not rise above the limit despite financial trends that are adverse to the lender).

capacity Measure of the ability of a company to produce goods or provide services. For a manufacturing business it is the amount produced in unit time, which may be expressed in direct labour hours, machine hours or standard hours.

capacity cost Fixed cost required to provide the means for a company to produce or sell, usually divided between enabling costs and standby costs.

capacity usage variance Variance forming part of the fixed overhead variance in standard costing. It is the gain or loss resulting from a difference between the budgeted hours and the actual hours worked. It is also known as the fixed overhead capacity variance or the idle capacity variance.

capacity variance Also called volume variance, the product of the standard fixed overhead rate per unit of (normal) capacity and the units of base activity budgeted for less the actual units of base activity that were worked during a given accounting period.

capital Imprecise term that, unqualified, generally refers to the resources of an organization or person (such as cash, equipment or skills), as contributed by the owners (i.e. the owners' equity). More precisely it is the total value of assets less liabilties.

capital account Account detailing how a company's share capital is distributed, or each partner's capital in a partnership.

capital allowance Amount deducted from a company's profits before tax is calculated, to take into account depreciation of capital assets (such as vehicles, plant and machinery, and industrial buildings).

capital assets Also sometimes called fixed assets, an imprecise term for such items as an organization's plant and equipment (tangible assets), goodwill (intangible asset) and investments.

capital asset pricing model (CAPM) Method of weighing risk and return to achieve the best equity value of a company in planning its financial policy.

capital budget Budget detailing proposed outgoings to obtain long-term assets, i.e. a company's capital expenditure. It involves longer timescales than a ***cash budget***. It is also known as a capital expenditure budget or capital investment budget.

capital costs Expenditure on capital goods, for example ***fixed assets*** such as plant, or on trade investments and ***current assets***. Capital costs are classed as below the line for accounting purposes. They are also known as capital expenditure, capital investment, investment costs or investment expenditure.

capital duty Former tax paid by UK companies on profits from new share issues. It ceased to be levied in 1988.

capital employed Capital that a company uses to finance its assets. It is taken to be the sum of the shareholders' funds, loans and deferred taxation.

capital expenditure Alternative term for ***capital costs.***

capital expenditure budget Alternative name for ***capital budget***.

capital fund Alternative term for ***accumulated fund***.

capital gain Gain made from a capital transaction, such as the buying and selling of assets. It is the amount by which the proceeds exceed the cost. *See also* ***chargeable assets***.

capital gains tax (CGT) Tax paid on *capital gains*. In the UK the rate of tax, which was introduced on 6 April 1965, depends on when the asset was acquired (before or after 31 March 1982 or after 6 April 1988). Rates of tax vary between 10% and 40%, depending on other income. Under US tax laws, a lower rate of capital gain tax is levied if the asset had been held for more than nine months before resale.

capital gearing Also called leverage, especially in the USA, the relationship between a company's funds derived from ordinary shares and long-term, fixed-interest rate funds such as preference shares and debentures. It is the ratio of the company's debts to total capital or shareholders' funds. High gearing, i.e. a high proportion of debt, generally represents a speculative investment.

capital instruments Any method employed to raise company finance (capital), such as debentures, loans, options and shares.

capital-intensive Describing a business in which capital is the most important and costly factor of production. For example, an industry in which the major cost is the purchase and maintenance of machinery (fixed assets) is capital-intensive. In times of recession, such businesses are generally viewed as speculative inventments.

capital investment Alternative name for *capital costs*.

capital investment budget Alternative name for *capital budget*.

capitalization Conversion of a company's reserves into share capital by issuing more shares (a scrip issue); or the total amount of capital available to a company in the long term; or the process of providing such capital.

capitalization of borrowing cost Cost of borrowing to buy a *fixed asset*.

capitalization of earnings Method of estimating a company's value by calculating the net present value of expected net income in the future.

capitalization rate Rate of interest employed in converting a series of amounts (such as earnings, payments or receipts) into a single present value.

capitalize To account for an expenditure such as that on advertising or research and development as an asset because it is expected to provide benefit in the future.

capital loss A negative *capital gain*, also called allowable capital loss.

capital maintenance concept Principle that a company's net assets at the end of a financial period should equal or exceed in value its net assets at the beginning of the period.

capital rationing Imposition of restraints on the amounts of total capital that can be spent in a given budgeted period.

capital profit Profit gained by selling an asset that was not purchased for resale originally.

capital redemption reserve Reserve created by a company's buying its own shares with a resulting lowering of share capital and maintenance of the capital base.

capital reserve Profits from a company's trading that are set aside as part of its capital and so may not be repaid to shareholders until the company is wound up.

capital risk In a lending situation, the risk that the investment's capital amount may be less than its par value (even when it matures).

capital structure Make-up of a company's borrowings in terms of the proportions of owners' equity, short-term debt and long-term debt. The complete financial structure includes also its assets and any other liabilities.

capital surplus Quantity more formally described as capital contributed in excess of par (stated) value. *See* ***surplus***.

capital turnover Ratio of revenue to employed capital.

CAMP Abbreviation of ***capital asset pricing model***.

captive finance company Finance company that is under the control of a commercial or industrial company.

CAR Abbreviation of ***compound annual return***.

carriage inwards Cost of delivery of purchased goods. If the purchase is of a ***fixed asset*** the carriage inwards may be capitalized on the balance sheet along with the asset.

carriage outwards Cost of delivery of goods sold. It is written off as a business expense to the profit and loss account.

carried down (c/d) Book-keeping term for an amount that is to be transferred as the next opening balance.

carried forward (c/f) Book-keeping term for a column total that is to be the opening figure in the corresponding column on the next page.

carrying amount Value of an asset or liability on a company's balance sheet, its ***book value***.

carrying cost Cost of holding or storing stock (inventory) from the time of purchase until used or re-sold. Such costs include insurance, rates, security and warehousing.

carrying value Alternative term for ***carrying amount***.

CASB Abbreviation of ***Cost Accounting Standards Board***.

cash Ready money (legal tender such as coins and notes), or to convert something (such as a cheque) into ready money.

cash accounting Also called cash-flow accounting (CFA), an accounting system that keeps records only of a business's cash transactions (receipts and payments), as opposed to ***accrual accounting*** which records when expenses are incurred or money is earned.

cash at bank Money deposited at a bank by a company or individual person. On a balance sheet it is listed under circulating assets.

cash basis Method of accounting in which expenses and revenue are accounted for only at the times that cash is received or disbursed. In this way it differs from the ***accrual basis***. *See also* ***cash collection basis***.

cash book In book-keeping, a book or journal in which all receipts and payments are recorded in the first instance. Entries are made in date order. *See also* ***cash receipts journal; cash payments journal***.

cash budget Forward plan of expected day-to-day income and expenditure. It is generally calculated monthly, and is also known as cash-flow budget, cash-flow forecast, cash-flow projection or financial budget.

cash collection basis Method of accounting in which revenue is identified in instalments, as it is received. *See also* ***cash basis***.

cash cow Product or aspect of business that continues to provide a healthy revenue after its initial launch, with relatively little extra investment.

cash cycle Time period during which cash is converted into stock (inventories), stock becomes accounts receivable, and receivables again become cash.

cash disbursements journal Journal in which payments of cash or by cheque are recorded. It is limited to cash only if there is also a cheque register.

cash discount Reduction in the price of goods or services in return for (prompt) payment in cash. Discounts allowed in this way are classified as expenditure. To the receiver of the discounts, they are regarded as revenue.

cash equivalent value Value of an asset in terms of the amount for which it could be sold; market value. The term is also applied to liquid investments that can rapidly be converted into cash.

cash float Money a salesperson or cashier has in order to be able to give change when customers' make purchases or cash cheques.

cash flow Movement of money through a company from when it is received as income (or borrowing), to the time it leaves the company as payments (for example, for raw material, wages, and so on). A negative cash flow occurs when there is too little money coming in to pay for all the outgoings. Conversely, a positive cash flow occurs when a company receives income before it is due to pay outgoings.

cash-flow accounting (CFA) Alternative name for ***cash accounting***.

cash-flow budget Alternative name for ***cash budget***

cash-flow forecast Alternative name for ***cash budget***.

cash-flow statement Statement detailing flows of cash and cash equivalents over a period, rather than of working capital as in a statement of changes in financial position.

cash flow to capital expenditure ratio Cash flows into a company divided by expenditure for fixed assets (plant and equipment). A ratio greater than one indicates that the company is self-financing.

cash flow to total debt ratio Cash flows into a company divided by total liabilities. A ratio of greater than one indicates that the company is solvent.

cash in hand Funds held as legal tender (coins and notes) as opposed to those deposited with a bank (cash at bank).

cash payments journal Journal that records sums paid out from a company's bank account.

cash receipts journal Journal that records receipts of cash into a company's bank account.

cash sale Sale made for cash, not on credit, and recorded in a cash payments journal.

cash to current liabilities ratio Company's cash and liquid securities

divided by its current liabilities. A ratio of greater than one indicates that the company can finance any short-term debts.

cash yield Company's cash flow divided by its book value.

CCA Abbreviation of ***current cost accounting***.

CCAB Abbreviation of ***Consultative Committee of Accountancy Bodies***.

CCE Abbreviation of ***current cash equivalent***.

ceiling Upper limit, particularly a borrowing limit (credit limit). In the USA, it is also an asset's ***net realizable value***.

central corporate expenses US term for general overhead expenses resulting from running a company's headquarters and its supporting structures. They are sometimes problematic in accounting terms.

Certificate in Management Accounting (CMA) US qualification awarded by the ***Institute of Management Accountants (IMA)***.

certificate of value Document that indicates whether or not stamp duty is payable. It certifies that a given transaction is not part of another transaction worth more than a certain value.

certified accountant (CA) Accountant who has passed the examinations of the Chartered Association of Certified Accountants.

certified financial statement In the USA, a financial statement that is attested to by an independent qualified auditor.

Certified Internal Auditor (CIA) In the USA, an auditor who has satisfied the requirements of the ***Institute of Internal Auditors (IIA)***.

Certified Management Accountant (CMA) In the USA, a management accountant who has passed the examinations of the ***Institute of Management Accountants (IMA)***.

Certified Public Accountant (CPA) In the USA, an accountant who has satisfied the requirement to be licensed by a state authority as a public accountant.

CFA Abbreviation of cost-flow accounting. *See* ***cash accounting***.

CGT Abbreviation of ***capital gains tax***.

chain discount US practice of quoting a series of discounts as percentages. For example, a chain discount of 10% and 5% is equivalent to 85.5% of list price (obtained by multiplying the list price by 0.90 and then by 0.95).

chairman's report Also known as the chairman's statement, a statement by a company's chairman (the most senior director) giving an account of the company's activities during a given financial period and possibly its plans for the immediate future. It is addressed to members of the company (i.e., shareholders), published in the annual report and accounts., and often read out by the chairman at the company's annual general meeting (AGM).

change fund US term for ***petty cash***, notes and coins issued to cashiers, shop sales staff and so on for giving change to customers.

changes in financial position Changes in the balances of cash or working capital during a financial period, as reflected in a company's accounts.

changes statement Statement of ***changes in financial position***.

charge Obligation to meet a debt, a debit to an account, or the process of debiting. It is also a legal interest in land agreed by a borrower to secure a loan that gives the chargee (often a bank or building society) a priority right to repayment when the land is sold. A creditor's interest in company property is also called charge and must be registered with the Registrar of Companies.

chargeable account period Period for which ***corporation tax*** is assessed, which must be less than a year.

chargeable assets All of a person's or company's property, unless defined as non-chargeable. For purposes of ***capital gains tax***, the following assets are exempted: cars, certain chattels, damages for injury, foreign currency (for private use), life assurance policies, main private residence, National Savings certificates, personal equity plan (PEP) investments, winnings from gambling and works of art.

chargeable event Any event or transaction that produces revenue that can be charged to ***capital gains tax*** or ***income tax***.

chargeable gain Any ***capital gain*** that results from disposing of an asset. *See* ***chargeable assets***.

chargeable person Anyone who was resident in the UK during the year in which he or she made a ***chargeable gain*** (and who is thereby liable to ***capital gains tax***).

chargeable transfer Gift that is liable to ***inheritance tax***.

charge account Type of ***credit account*** that provides extended credit to a shop's customers. A retailer offering such a facility must hold a licence to do so.

charge and discharge accounting Historical type of accounting used in the Middle Ages. A person charged himself with estate or sums he should receive, and credited himself with any sums paid out.

charge off Alternative term for ***write off***; i.e., to regard an amount originally recorded as an asset as an expense or loss.

charges forward When goods are to be delivered, a notice that all carriage charges must be paid at the time the goods are delivered.

charity accounts Special accounting method that has to be used by registered charities (under the Charities Act (1993)). It requires that all receipts (from fund-raising activities, donations, grants and legacies) and all outgoings (such as expenses and donations and grants made) should be shown in detail.

chartered accountant (CA) In England and Wales, an accountant who has passed the examinations of the Institute of Chartered Accountants and is either an associate or fellow of the Institute. In Ireland and Scotland, a chartered accountant is an associate or fellow of the Institute of Chartered Accountants in Ireland, and Scotland, respectively. Similar methods of qualification are used in Australia and Canada, although in Canada individual provinces retain a say (and examinations may be in French). The main difference between a chartered accountant and a ***certified accountant*** is that the training of the former usually involves a period of time working with a firm of accountants and that of the latter does not.

Chartered Association of Certified Accountants Organization established in 1938 as the Association of Certified and Corporate Accountants, itself resulting from a merger of the Corporation of Accountants (founded 1891) and the London Association of Accountants (founded in 1904). The Institute of Certified Public Accountants joined in 1941 when the organization received its present name.

Chartered Institute of Management Accountants (CIMA) Organization established in 1919, originally as the Institute of Cost and Works Accountants.

Chartered Institute of Public Finance and Accountancy (CIPFA) Organization established in 1885, originally as the Corporate Treasurers and Accountants Institute.

Chartered Institute of Taxation Until 1994 the Institute of Taxation, an organization whose members work in various firms, dealing with taxation matters.

chart of accounts List showing how of all of an organizations various accounts are classified. *See also* ***account code***.

choice criterion Alternative US term for ***objective function***.

CIA Abbreviation of ***Certified Internal Auditor***.

CICA Abbreviation of ***Canadian Institute of Chartered Accountants***.

CIMA Abbreviation of ***Chartered Institute of Management Accountants***.

CIPFA Abbreviation of ***Chartered Institute of Public Finance and Accountancy***.

circularization of debtors Auditing method in which all of a company's debtors are asked either to confirm that a stated amount is in dispute or incorrect (called negative cicularization), or to confirm that the stated amount is correct (positive circularization).

circulating assets Money used for a company to invest in assets for resale. When such assets have been sold, the capital raised returns to the company. They are also called circulating capital, current assets or floating assets.

circulating capital Alternative term for ***circulating assets.***

clean opinion Unqualified auditor's report on the financial affairs of a company.

clean surplus concept In contrast to the formerly used ***current operating performance concept***, a US accounting method in which only net earnings and dividends are entered into the ***retained earnings*** account.

clearing account Account that details sums to be transferred to another account at the end of the accounting period.

clock card Also called a time card, a card on which an employee's time at work or time on a particular job is recorded. It is usually marked by a mechanical clock mechanism or electronically.

close To transfer the balance of an ***adjunct account***, ***contra account*** or ***temporary account*** to the main account it relates to.

closed account Account on which credits equal debits, usually because a ***closing entry*** has been made.

closed-end fund Fund with fixed capital, as opposed to an open-ended fund. Sums held by investment companies are closed-end funds (investment trusts).

closing balance At the end of an accounting period, the credit or debit balance on a ledger. It is carried forward to the next accounting period (credits to the debit side and debits to the credit side).

closing entry At the end of an accounting period, a final entry made to close off expense and income ledgers (which are transferred to the profit and loss account).

closing inventory Also called ending inventory, US term for the value of stock in hand at the end of an accounting period (which is carried over to the next period). *See also* ***closing stock***.

closing-rate method Way of restating balance sheet figures in another currency using the rate of exchange quoted at the end of the day on the balance sheet date.

closing stock Stock that remains at the end of an accounting period. It may be in the form of finished goods, work in progress or raw materials. Their value appears on the balance sheet under ***circulating assets***.

cluster sampling Auditing technique in which a population (of, say, receipts or invoices) is divided into clusters and a random sample taken from each.

CMA Abbreviation of ***Certificate in Management Accounting*** and ***Certified Management Accountant***.

CNAR Abbreviation of ***compound net annual rate***.

CoCoA Abbreviation of ***continuously contemporary accounting***.

coding of accounts *See* ***account code***.

COGS Abbreviation of ***cost of goods sold***.

collar In return for a premium, an option that guarantees a borrower a fixed maximum interest (cap) and fixed minimum interest (floor) for a loan.

collateral Alternative term for ***security*** put up for a loan.

collateralize US term for pledging assets to secure a loan.

collectible Item acquired for possible resale to make a ***capital gain*** (as well as for its aesthetic value). Examples include antiques, postage stamps, works of art and even vintage cars. In the USA, the term is often applied to anything that can be converted into cash.

collection period Time it takes to collect payment of a debt (reckoned in days, weeks or even months).

columnar accounts Accounts that are drawn up in several vertical columns.

combined financial statement In US practice, the bringing together of the financial statements of a group of related companies or cost centres to show financial information for the group as a whole, as if it were a single entity.

commission Money paid to an agent or other intermediary, usually as a percentage of the sum involved in the transaction.

commission agent Agent who is paid a ***commission***, usually calculated as a percentage of the value of purchases or sales made overseas.

commissions paid account Account in which a company details commissions paid to agents or other intermediaries.

commissions received account Account in which a company records commissions received for acting as an agent or other intermediary.

commitments for capital expenditure Future commitments a company has to spend on fixed assets, as revealed in its accounts.

committed costs Long-term fixed costs that a company has committed to pay, such as rent or ***depreciation*** on a long-lived asset. Some of these costs may vary with the volume of production.

Committee on Accounting for Smaller Entities Committee of the *Accounting Standards Board (ASB)* that advises on accounting standards as they apply to smaller organizations.

Committee on Accounting Procedure In the USA from 1939 to 1959, a committee of the American Institute of Certified Public Accountants. It published 51 *Accounting Research Bulletins* before being superseded by the *Accounting Principles Board (APB)*.

commodity code Code assigned to each material or product (used or produced) within a company so that it can be recorded in various control systems.

common cost Cost that provides benefit to more than one department or product of a company and which should therefore be shared among them. Such costs may relate to raw materials, services (such as insurance) and facilities (such as plant and machinery). *See also* ***joint costs***.

common-dollar accounting US term for ***price-level accounting***.

common monetary measuring unit Usual local currency – in the UK, the pound sterling and in the USA the American dollar.

common-size statement Method of analysis that uses percentages to express elements in financial statements so that they may easily be compared.

Companies House Informal name of ***Companies Registration Office***.

Companies Registration Office Known informally as Companies House, the location of the office of the Registrar of Companies, in Cardiff, Wales. It contains a register of all UK companies, listing the names of its directors and shareholders as well as copies of its latest balance sheet.

company auditor Person appointed to audit a company's accounts, who must be a registered auditor, in accordance with the requirements of the Companies Act.

company secretary Person who is responsible for ensuring that his or her company complies with company law. He or she is an officer of the company but need not be a director.

comparative figures In a company's financial statements, figures for earlier years, included for the purposes of comparison. The previous year's figures, at least, are a legal requirement. They are also called, especially in the USA, comparative statements.

comparative statements *See* ***comparative figures***.

compensating error Error undetected in a trial balance because it has been cancelled out by another error (or errors).

compilation report Former name for an ***audit exemption*** report.

completed contract method Method of accounting in which long-term revenues and expenses are recognized only when a job or order is completed. If a loss is anticipated, it is recognized in the period in which the loss is first forecast. *See also* ***completed sales method***.

completed sales method Method of accounting for sales revenue only when a sale has been delivered and payment received. It is equivalent to a short-term ***completed contract method***.

compliance audit Audit to establish that internal control procedures are being complied with.

compliance tests Tests employed in a ***compliance audit***.

composite life method Method of calculating ***depreciation*** of an item of plant or machinery in its entirety, rather than accounting for the separate depreciation of each component. For example, instead of depreciating a vehicle's engine, transmission, chassis, and so on separately, the vehicle as a whole is depreciated. It is a type of ***group depreciation***.

component percentages *See* ***common-size statement***.

compound annual return (CAR) Total return on a sum invested or lent over a period of a year, including the return on interest previously accrued. *See also* ***compound net annual rate (CNAR)***.

compound entry Journal entry that has more than one credit or debit (as when an asset is traded in for a new one, for example).

compound discount Difference between today's discounted value of an amount and its worth in the future.

compound interest Rate of interest calculated by adding interest previously paid to the capital sum plus previous interest payment. After n years a sum S invested at x per cent compound interest is worth $S[(100 + n)/100]^n$. *See also* ***simple interest***.

compound net annual rate (CNAR) Return, after deduction of tax at the basic rate, of interest from a deposit or investment that includes the return of interest previously accrued. *See also* ***compound annual return***.

compounding period Period of time over which ***compound interest*** is calculated.

comprehensive annual financial report (CAFR) Official annual report of the American government.

comprehensive auditing Auditing of the accounts of a government department or a non-profit making organization such as a charity to ensure that it operates efficiently, giving value for the money it utilizes. It is also known as a value-for-money audit.

comprehensive budget Budget that coordinates and forecasts every financial statement and their individual items for the whole of an organization. It thus represents the organization's overall plans for the future. It is also known as a master budget.

comprehensive income For a given accounting period, the sum of a company's holding gains (increase in the value of assets) and operating profits (excess of operating income over expenditure).

comptroller Mainly US term for the chief financial officer of a group of companies or the financial director of a single company. The title should not be confused with that of controller, who is the chief accounting executive, although not all companies preserve the distinction. Both titles are pronounced in the same manner.

computer-assisted audit technique (CAAT) When a company's financial records are held on computer files, an auditing method that employs a computerized system for performing compliance tests and substantive tests.

conceptual framework In the UK, the ***Statement of Principles*** issued by the ***Accounting Standards Board (ASB)***; in the USA, the ***Statement of Financial Accounting Concepts (SFAC)*** as issued by the ***Financial Accounting Standards Board (FASB)***. They both provide theoretical guidelines for accounting and financial reporting.

conditional value Value that results if a specified event occurs (or does not occur). For example, the value of a piece of equipment may depend on whether or not it is free from rust when it comes to be sold.

confirmation Method an auditor uses to get evidence from a third party of the accuracy of information provided by a client. A positive confirmation is requested whether the balance figure, for example, is correct or incorrect. The return of a negative confirmation is requested only in the event that the figures are incorrect.

conservatism Accounting concept requiring that all possible expenses and losses should be anticipated, but that no gains or profits should be recognized until they are actually realized. It is the US equivalent of the UK ***prudence concept***.

consignee Person or company to which goods are sent.

consignment Shipment of goods sent or delivered at the same time, usually to an agent for selling on to somebody else (the consignee). *See also* ***on consignment***.

consignment note Document sent with a consignment of goods, to be signed by the consignee or his agent upon receipt of the goods. It may also be known as a waybill.

consignment stock Stock held by an agent or dealer that legally belongs to somebody else. The dealer can, in law, sell it or return it unsold to the rightful owner.

consignor Person or company that dispatches goods (to a consignee).

consistency concept In accounting, a concept whereby accounts for one accounting period are constructed on the same principles as for another period.

consolidated accounts Combined financial statements of a group of subsidiary companies. Although each member of the group has its own profit and loss accounts, these must be consolidated to form accounts for the whole group, as required by the Companies Act. They are also called consolidated financial statements, group accounts or group financial statements.

consolidated balance sheet Balance sheet of a group of companies which contains financial details of the subsidiaries, combined with those of the parent company. *See* ***consolidated accounts***.

consolidated cash-flow statement Result of consolidating the cash-flow statements of a group of subsidiary companies with that of the parent company.

consolidated financial statements Alternative term for ***consolidated accounts.***

consolidated income and expenditure account Individual information from the income and expenditure accounts of a group of subsidiary companies consolidated with that of the parent company.

consolidated profit Combined profit of the members of a group of subsidiary companies, as recorded in the ***consolidated profit and loss account***.

consolidated profit and loss account Result of consolidating the individual profit and loss accounts of a group of subsidiary companies (although that of the parent company need not be included, but this fact must be stated).

consolidation Practice of putting together the individual accounts of subsidiary companies of a group, to calculate overall results for the group as a whole.

consolidation adjustments Certain adjustments that are made during the ***consolidation*** of subsidiary companies' accounts. For example, any profit or loss from transactions between members of the group are excluded.

constant dollar accounting US term for the use of a currency unit of constant purchasing power in the historical costing of assets in a financial statement. Reference is made to consumer price indexes in arriving at the value. It is also termed ***current cost accounting***.

constant purchasing power accounting Also called current purchasing power (CPP) accounting, method of accounting that allows for the constancy of the purchasing power of shareholders' capital before measuring profit. General price changes are adjusted in line with the Retail Price Index. It is similar to the US method of ***constant dollar accounting***.

constraint Something that prevents an organization from performing better. It may be a shortage of such things as labour, production capacity or raw materials, which must be remedied before performance levels can improve.

constructive receipt In US tax regulations, income over which the recipient has control whether or not cash has been received (such as interest on a savings account).

Consultative Committee of Accountancy Bodies (CCAB) Organization founded in 1970 to encourage closer cooperation between the six UK accountancy bodies: the Chartered Association of Certified Accountants, Chartered Institute of Management Accountants, Chartered Institute of Public Finance and Accountancy, Institute of Chartered Accountants in England and Wales, Institute of Chartered Accountants in Ireland, and Institute of Chartered Accountants in Scotland.

consumable material Material that is used up in producing something, although not part of the prime cost (as is a ***direct material***), such as abrasives, cleaning agents and lubricating oil.

Consumer Price Index Measure of price levels calculated in the USA by the Bureau of Labor Statistics (using the year 1967 as a base). See also ***Retail Price Index.***

contingency Allowance for a possible loss (or gain) written into a costing or account. The prudence concept requires that contingent losses, particularly, should be disclosed.

contingency theory of management accounting Thesis that there is no one management accounting system that suits all organizations or even all circumstances in a single organization. For this reason, the system has to be contingent on the prevailing conditions and adaptable to meet changes in these conditions.

contingent agreement *See* ***earn-out***.

contingent asset Asset that may arise, depending on some contingency – i.e., because of what has happened in the past but cannot be guaranteed nor confirmed until something else happens (which is not under the total control of the entity concerned).

contingent gain Gain that may arise, depending on some contingency. *See* ***contingent asset***.

contingent issue Describing securities that are issued to certain people depending on some contingency (such as a specified amount of profit).

contingent liability Liability that may arise, depending on some contingency. *See also* ***contingent gain***.

contingent loss Loss that may arise, depending on some contingency. *See also* ***contingent gain.***

continuing appropriation In the USA, a government appropriation that is reviewed automatically from time to time (unless expended or revoked).

continuity convention *See* ***continuity of operations***.

continuity of operations Assumption in company accounting that an organization is a going concern, i.e., that it will continue trading for current plans to be completed. It is also known as the continuity convention.

continuous budget Budget to which a month (or quarter) is continually added as the current month (or quarter) expires.

continuous compounding Method of calculating ***compound interest*** in which the compounding period is taken to be every instant of time. If interest is compounded at a rate of r per period, the effective interest rate is the same as interest compounded once per period at a rate of i, where $i = e^r - 1$ (and e is the base of natural logarithms).

continuous inventory Also called perpetual inventory, continuous audit or continuous stocktaking, a way of keeping a record of stock which is changed whenever an item is added to or removed from the stock. It is most commonly used in retailing, where stock turnover is fast.

continuously contemporary accounting (CoCoA) Method of accounting that takes into account general changes in price levels, indicating whether or not an organization can modify its policies in a changing environment. A theoretical concept by the Australian Raymond J. Chambers, it has found much more favour with academics than with practical accountants.

continuous-operation costing Costing method used by companies that operate a continuous production process (such as power generation or steel-making). The total production cost is divided by the number of items (or amount of product) produced to give an average unit cost.

continuous stocktaking *See* ***continuous inventory***.

contra Latin for 'opposite side', used of book-keeping entries that are on the opposite side of an account to earlier entries, which they effectively cancel out. *See also* ***per contra***.

contra account Account that is credited or debited against another account. Contra accounts can thus be offset against each other. Allowances for bad debts and accumulated depreciation are typical contra accounts.

contract costing Method of costing used for long-term contracts where costs are recovered from contract payments. Work in progress may have to valued at the end of the financial year to determine the amount of profit, to be taken into the profit and loss account.

contributed capital US term for the sum of the contributed surplus (capital contributed in excess of stated value) and capital stock (shares), as opposed the capital derived from retained income.

contributed surplus US term for the amount received by an issuer for capital stock (shares) in excess of the stated (par) value.

contribution Money earned or paid in addition to another sum, often used to describe extra profit that accrues once a product's break-even point has been reached.

contribution approach Way of drawing up an income statement (or profit and loss account) in which fixed costs are separated from variable costs to reveal the cost behaviour pattern, and thus facilitate cost control. Unlike absorption costing, fixed costs are not charged to individual products but listed as a deduction from all products' total contribution.

contribution margin Also called marginal contribution, the sum remaining when variable expenses are deducted from sales revenue. It may be expressed per unit, as a total, as a percentage or, more often, as a ratio (contribution-to-sales ratio, production-volume ratio). In this way, products may be listed in order of profitability.

contribution per unit Contribution margin expressed per unit.

control account Also called controlling account, an account whose totals equal balances that appear in individual accounts in subsidiary ledgers.

control budget variance Also called flexible budget variance, the difference between actual amounts and flexible-budget amounts for the output produced.

control factor unit Method of measuring someone's workload (such as items mailed per day or calls answered per hour).

controllable cost Cost (fixed or variable) that management can directly control, either in the short or long term. Advertising costs are an example.

controllable variance Variance (in budgetary control or standard costing) that management can directly control. It arises through differences between budgeted cost and the actual cost incurred (in a given period).

controller *See* ***comptroller***.

control period Time during which actual results (outgoings or revenue) are compared with their budgeted equivalents. The exercise may be done several times during a financial year (typically monthly or quarterly) to facilitate budgetary control.

control risk Risk that a company's internal control systems will not detect or prevent an error in its financial statements.

control system Any method applied to single functions within a company (operational control), to autonomous sectors within it (divisional control) or to the company as a whole (company-wide control) to ensure that activities correspond to those that were planned.

conversion cost Sum of the direct labour cost and overheads involved in producing a product (but excluding the cost of raw materials).

cooking the books Slang expression for falsifying financial records or statements to mislead others.

co-product Product that uses the same production facilties as another one (such as clothing). *See also* ***by-product; joint product***.

corporate failure prediction Method of predicting whether or not a company will go into liquidation. There are various models which produce scores that indicate probable success or failure.

corporation tax (CT) Tax levied on a UK company's profits. The rate depends on the amount of profit, starting at 10% for companies whose profits are less than £10,000, rising to 20% for companies with profits of between £10,000 and £300,000, rising to 30% for companies making more than $1.5 million. *See also* ***advance corporation tax***.

correcting entry Entry on an account that corrects a previous error.

corresponding amount Amount in a company's accounts that relates to the previous financial year, as required by the Companies Act.

COSA Abbreviation of ***cost of sales adjustment***.

cost Amount of money that has to be expended to acquire something (goods or services), in most cases its price. A company's costs may be defined in a number of ways, such as acquisition cost, average cost, historical cost and replacement cost. *See also* ***fixed cost; variable cost.***

cost absorption *See* ***absorption costing***.

cost accountant Accountant who specializes in reckoning the cost of manufacturing a unit of product, taking into account such variables as cost of raw materials and labour, and thereby making a projection of probable cost at the planning stage of a project. This, in turn, can enable a manufacturer to tender a price to a prospective buyer. It is usually regarded as an area within management accounting.

cost accounting Activities of a ***cost accountant***.

Cost Accounting Standards Board (CASB) Board of five members, founded by Congress in the USA in 1970, which sought to establish consistency and uniformity in the cost accounting principles applied to government contracts. In 1980 it was superseded by a department of the Government Accounting Office.

cost accumulation Use of an accounting system to collect costs in some organized manner, usually as a product moves through a production process.

cost allocation Assignment of a cost (or a group of costs) to one or more ***cost centres*** which directly incur that cost.

cost-allocation base Common factor used in tracing a particular cost or costs to the ***cost centres***, such as machine-hours or direct-labour-hours.

cost application Alternative term for cost absorption. *See* ***absorption costing***.

cost apportionment *See* ***apportionment***.

cost approximation Also called cost estimation, the process of employing estimated unit costs for direct costs and overheads in order to estimate the cost of an item (product or service).

cost ascertainment Process of finding costs within a company (e.g., of operations and processes).

C

cost attribution Method by which cost centres are made to pay or be responsible for costs, which then go towards determining the price charged for goods or services.

cost behaviour pattern Pattern of changes in cost that result from changes in the level of a company's activities. Variable costs tend to rise or fall, although fixed costs may remain largely unchanged in the short term.

cost-benefit criterion Principle that, if a system is changed, its additional benefits should exceed its addition costs.

cost centre Specific operation within an organization that is charged separately for its own expenses (so that its costs can be accurately assessed).

cost classification Method of finding common characteristics so that expenses can be placed in groups. The first major grouping is usually into capital costs and revenue costs. Each of these can then be broken down into, for example, material, labour and overhead costs. Overheads can be further subdivided into those arising from administration, distribution, production, research and sales, and so on.

cost code Alternative term for ***account code***.

cost control Methods employed to ensure that costs within an organization remain at acceptable levels.

cost control account Type of control account in a system that has different accounts for costing and financial records. The cost control account balance is the same as the total of entries in the cost ledger. It is therefore also sometimes called a cost ledger control account.

cost convention Current cost, historical cost or replacement cost, used as a basis for recording items charged against profit for a given accounting period.

cost driver Anything that happens in a company that incurs cost. Activity-based costing uses such drivers to assign cost to particular products or services.

cost effective Describing something that gives value for money. As a relative term, it is used of an activity that has the greatest ratio of revenue (or benefit) to cost (among alternative activities).

cost estimation Alternative term for ***cost approximation***.

cost flow Cost that passes through various definable parts of an entity.

cost function Relationship between cost and one or more variable quantities. A common example is $y = a + bx$, where y is total cost, a is total fixed cost, b is variable cost per unit and x is the number of units produced. Another equation could be constructed to relate the cost of repairs to a machine in terms of the number of hours it had been in use or the amount of product it had produced.

costing Practice of working out how much a product will cost to produce, taking into account costs such as raw materials, labour, overheads, and so on. A frequent alternative term is costing-out.

costing method Any method, such as absorption costing or process costing, employed in ***cost accounting*** to determine the costs of processes, products and services within a company.

cost item Group of costs of a similar type, such as consumables and cost of sales, usually brought together within a company and treated as a single item by the costing system.

cost ledger Account book in which cost accounting records are kept.

cost ledger control account Alternative name for a ***cost control account***.

cost objective Any activity whose costs are measured separately. The term is also sometimes used as a synonym of ***cost centre***.

cost of capital Average annual interest rate that a company pays for its working capital. It may consist of equity shares, loans and debt. The term is also used to mean the required rate of return on an investment.

cost of goods manufactured Within a given accounting period, the total expenditure on producing products during the period, including the costs of materials, labour and overheads. Adjustments may have to be made for work in progress and stocks at the beginning and end of the period.

cost of goods purchased Expenditure on goods purchased, including costs of delivery and storage until they are used.

cost of goods sold (COGS) Cost of items that are produced (or bought) and then sold (or resold). For a given accounting period, it is the value of stock at the beginning of the period plus the cost of goods produced (or bought) minus the value of stock at the end of the period.

cost of sales Usually the expense incurred in making sales (such as the cost of advertising, wages of sales personnel, and so on). The term is also sometimes used to mean the ***cost of goods sold***.

cost of sale adjustment (COSA) In current cost accounting, an adjustment to a company's trading profit because there is a ***holding gain*** on the cost of items sold.

cost percentage Percentage equal to 1 minus the markup percentage. In FIFO stock-keeping (***first in first out***), it is the ratio of cost of goods available for sale and the selling price of goods available for sale. In the LIFO method (***last in first out***), it is the ratio of the cost of purchases and the selling price.

cost-plus contract Type of sales contract under the terms of which a supplier of goods or services charges cost price plus an agreed percentage markup.

cost-plus pricing Method of pricing in which the buyer pays the cost of an item plus a commission to the seller, as with a ***cost-plus contract***. The term is also applied to a method of arriving at the selling price of goods or services by estimating the total cost to produce or provide them and then adding a percentage markup in order to make a profit.

cost pool Group of separate costs that are assigned as a single item to a product, such as handling costs allocated in terms of the amount of material handled.

cost prediction Using a knowledge of how costs behaved in the past to statistically estimate future costs.

cost principle Accounting principle which requires that assets be recorded at acquisition or historical cost minus accumulated amortization. It assumes that later changes are not significant and that fair market value was paid in the first instance.

cost-recovery first method Method of recording revenue that recognizes it as income only after all costs have been recovered.

cost sheet Statement detailing all the elements that contribute to the total cost of an item (such as goods, processes, services or even a cost centre).

cost-to-cost Type of ***percentage of completion*** in which the estimate of completion is taken as costs incurred so far divided by the estimated total costs of the whole project.

cost unit Single item to which a cost may be ascribed for accounting purposes. Cost units may include simple articles such as raw materials (e.g., a plank of wood) or completed items (such as a table), or articles in production (although these are more complicated because they require the accounting to take into account direct and indirect costs). When items are small, the cost unit may be a production batch. *See also* ***cost centre***.

cost-volume-profit analysis Alternative term for ***breakeven analysis***.

council tax Local-government UK tax levied on property according to its market value, with a lower level of tax for buildings with only one occupant. It was established in 1993-94 (when it replaced the community charge).

countervailing credit Alternative term for ***back-to-back credit***.

CPA Abbreviation of ***Certified Public Accountant***.

CPP Abbreviation of current purchasing power. *See* ***constant purchasing power accounting***.

creative accounting Also known informally as number fudging or window dressing, the creation of a favourable account sheet without resort to actual fraud. *See*, for example, ***income smoothing***.

credit Loan of money (made by a trader before requiring payment for goods or services), or a book-keeping balance that shows a profit (i.e., on the right-hand side of the account), or a person's or company's financial standing, or to add a sum to an account.

credit account Also called a charge account, an account offered by some retail stores and chains which allows a customer to purchase goods on the spot (usually by means of a plastic card) and to pay for them at the end of the accounting period or in instalments. Some credit accounts also charge interest.

credit balance Account balance showing that more money has been received than has been debited, and so the account concerned is in credit.

credit control Method employed by a company to ensure that its debts are paid within a reasonable time.

credit entry Item recorded in a ledger (on the right-hand side) for accounting purposes. It represents an expense or decrease in the value of an asset, or an increase in equity, liability or revenue.

credit loss Bad debts; the amount of accounts receivable that is expected to be uncollectible.

credit memorandum Document, drawn up by a seller, that informs a buyer that his or her account receivable is being reduced (credited). The reason might be because of an allowance, an error or a return.

credit note Document, sometimes printed in red ink, issued to confirm the transfer of credit from one account to another. The term is also used for a note or document that confirms the availability of funds for future purchases.

creditor Person or company that lends or is owed money. In company accounting, creditors who are due to be paid within a year are classified as current creditors; creditors who are not due to be paid until after a year are classified as long-term liabilities.

creditor-days ratio Estimate of the average time a company takes to pay its creditors. It is equal to 365 times the number of trade creditors divided by the number of purchases made on credit in a year.

creditors' buffer Fixed capital base of a company (which cannot normally be touched). Its existence provides confidence for short-term creditors and long-term debenture holders.

creditors' ledger Also called a purchases ledger, a ledger that details individual creditor's accounts.

creditors' ledger control account Also called purchases ledger control account, a ledger control account that details totals from entries in the creditors' ledgers from the payments and purchases journals.

credit rating Rating assigned to a person or company that assesses creditworthiness.

credit risk When a loan is made, the risk that the borrower will be unable (or unwilling) to repay the principal and any interest owing.

credit sale Purchase that is paid for at a future date, possibly in instalments.

creditworthiness Assessment of a person's or company's ability to pay for goods or services. It may be expressed as a credit rating.

cross-reference index Method of keeping track of book-keeping entries by assigning a number to each account in a journal entry which indicates the ledger entry to which it is posted. The page number of the journal in which the entry is made is recorded in the ledger. In this way, credit and debit elements of a ledger account can be traced back to the original journal entry.

cross-section analysis Analysis of various companies' financial statements for a single accounting period (as opposed to time-series analysis, in which a single company's statements are analysed over several time periods).

CT Abbreviation of ***corporation tax***.

current accounts In company accounting, an account detailing interdepartmental or intercompany balances, or an account detailing transactions of a partner in a partnership which do not relate to his or her capital. *See also* ***capital account***.

current assets Alternative name for ***circulating assets***.

current assets ratio Total of current assets, including stock-in-trade, divided by total of current liabilities. A test of a company's liquidity, it is also known as current ratio and working-capital ratio.

current cash equivalent (CCE) Measure of assets and liabilities in ***continuously contemporary accounting***.

current cost Cost (e.g., of an asset) stated in terms of current market prices (as opposed to acquisition cost).

current cost accounting (CCA) Also known as inflation accounting, a method of accounting that takes changes in pricing due to inflation into account, adjusting the values of assets, costs, and so on. *See also* ***constant dollar accounting***.

current-cost depreciation Depreciation charge based on the current cost of assets (as opposed to acquisition or historical cost).

current-cost method *See* ***current cost accounting***.

current-cost operating profit In the current cost accounting method, the amount that is left after the accounting profit has had various adjustments made to it (such as depreciation adjustment and sales adjustment).

current expenditure Expenditure on assets for resale (such as raw materials), rather than on fixed assets. It is also known as above-the-line expenditure.

current fund In the USA, an alternative term for the ***general fund*** of the government.

current liability Money owed by a person or company that should be paid within a year of the date of the balance sheet (as opposed to a long-term liability).

current gross margin Also called operating margin, sales revenues less current replacement cost of goods sold. It provides a measure of operating efficiency without any cost-flow assumptions for stock.

current operating performance concept Former concept in the USA which expected that income for a period should reflect only ordinary recurring operations of that period. As a result, extraordinary and nonrecurring items had to be recorded directly in the retained earnings account.

current purchasing power (CPP) accounting Alternative term for *constant purchasing power accounting*.

current ratio Alternative term for *current assets ratio*.

current replacement cost For a particular asset, the lower of the current cost of an identical replacement or of one that could do the same job.

current selling price Amount that could be obtained for an asset in an arm's length transaction (i.e., not in a forced sale).

current standard In standard costing, a cost, income or performance standard related to current operations, to be used over a short time span.

current value accounting Method of accounting in which assets are shown at current replacement cost, net present value or net realizable value and liabilities are shown at present value.

current-year basis Method of charging taxes in a fiscal year (April to April) on profits accounted for in the period ending in that year.

customers' ledger Ledger detailing accounts receivable of a company's individual customers.

cut-off date Date at the end of a company's accounting period, when the accounts are ruled off.

cut-off rate Minimum required rate of return on an activity or investment.

cycle billing Method of invoicing a company's creditors at different time intervals, which tends to even out work load and cash flow.

D

dangling debit Former method by means of which a company creates a goodwill account by writing off goodwill to reserves. Funds in a goodwill account are excluded from shareholders' funds. The practice is no longer permitted.

day book Ledger (a book of prime entry) in which transactions are listed on a daily basis before being transferred into ledgers that deal with transactions on a subject basis. It is customary to keep separate purchase and sales day books.

days of average inventory on hand US term for a ratio equal to 365 divided by inventory (stock) turnover.

days' sales in inventory Estimate of how long present stocks will last, equal to the amount of inventory (stock) stated in terms of days of sales. For instance, if 40 items are held in stock and 5 are sold each day, it is equal to 40 ÷ 5 = 8 days' sales in inventory.

days' sales in receivables Amount of receivables stated in terms of days of sales. For instance, if the receivables (i.e., debtors) outstanding total £40,000 and £2000 worth of sales are made daily, it is equal to $40,000 ÷ £2000 = 20 days' sales in receivables.

days' sales outstanding Amount of outstanding sales stated in terms of days. For instance, if £40,000 worth of sales are outstanding and £2500 worth of sales are made daily, it is equal to £40,000 ÷ £2500 = 16 days' sales outstanding.

DCF Abbreviation of ***discounted cash flow***.

DCV Abbreviation of ***direct charge voucher***.

Dearing Report Report called *The Making of Accounting Standards*, published in 1988. It was produced by a committee chaired by Sir Ronald Dearing and resulted in the establishment of the ***Accounting Standards Board*** (ASB) to replace the Accounting Standards Committee.

death duty Also called estate duty, a former tax levied in the UK until 1975 on the estate of someone who has died. It was superseded by capital transfer tax, which was itself replaced in 1986 by ***inheritance tax***.

debenture redemption reserve Capital reserve account established by a company to hold funds for the future redemption of debentures. The funds are transferred from the profit and loss account, thus reducing the amount of profits payable in dividends to ordinary shareholders.

debit Sum owed by or a charge made on a person or organization. In double-entry book-keeping, a debit appears on the left-hand side of an account, where it represents an increase in assets or expenditure (corresponding to a decrease in liabilities, owners' equities or revenues). *See* ***debt and credit rules***.

debit and credit conventions Equal amounts of credits and debits have to be recorded for each transaction in order to maintain the equality of the sides of the accounting equation.

debit balance Balance that shows a debit (i.e., the sum of the credit entries is less than the sum of the debit entries).

debit entry In double-entry book-keeping, an entry made on the left-hand side of an account. *See* ***debit***.

debit memorandum Document issued by a seller to notify a buyer that his or her account receivable is being increased (i.e., is being debited) because of an error.

debit note Notification sent to a customer that a supplier is about the debit the client's account with a certain sum. Debit notes are normally issued only in unusual circumstances, as when the client has been charged too little for goods or services delivered.

debt Sum of money, or value of goods or services, owed by one person, group or company to another. Debts arise because the seller allows the purchaser ***credit***. Assignable debts may be transferred in whole from one person to another. In commerce, especially in the USA, the term is also used to describe the whole of a company's long-term borrowings.

debt and credit rules In double-entry book-keeping, a set of rules relating to how debits and credits should be entered into an account. A debit entry increases an asset account and a credit entry decreases it. A debit entry decreases a capital account and a credit entry increases it. A debit entry increases an expense account and a credit entry decreases it. A debit entry decreases a liability account and a credit entry increases it. And a debit entry decreases a revenue account and a credit entry increases it.

debt capital Another name for ***borrowed capital***.

D

debt discounting Purchasing a debt at a discount, usually from a trader such as an importer.

debt-equity ratio In its simplest terms, a company's total liabilities (long-term debt) divided by its total equities. It gives an indication of a company's ***gearing***.

debt factoring Purchasing of a company's debts (at a discount) by a factor (*see* ***factoring***).

debt financing Method a company uses to raise funds, by issuing bonds, mortgages or notes.

debt-for-equity Substitution of an equity stake for a debt that is proving difficult to recover, despite the good prospects of the borrower.

debt forgiveness In international finance, writing off part of a nation's debt, or selling the debt to a third party for a large discount.

debt instrument Document that details the terms and conditions that apply to a short-term loan.

debtor (dr) Person or company that owes money, goods or services to another. Individual accounts are kept in a ***debtors' ledger***.

debtor collection period Average time it takes a company to collect money it is owed (including any credit period). It is also known as the average collection period.

debtors' ledger Also known as the sales ledger or sold ledger, a ledger account that details individual debtor accounts, whose total should agree with that of the ***debtors' ledger control account***.

debtors' ledger control account General ledger control account that details the totals transferred from the cash receipts journal and the sales day book to individual ***debtors' ledgers***. It is also known as the sales ledger control account.

debt ratio Alternative US term for ***debt-equity ratio***.

debt rescheduling When a debtor has difficulties making repayments, a method by which the lender defers interest or repayments, extends the loan period, or agrees to a completely new loan.

debt service fund In US government accounting, a special fund that accounts for repayments (principal and interest) of all general obligation debt (except those paid from special assessments).

debt service requirement In the USA, money needed for paying principal, interest and outstanding debts as well as, in the case of companies, to a sinking fund or (in the case of government organizations) to the ***debt service fund***.

debt servicing Payment of interest on a debt.

debt-to-equity ratio *See* ***debt-equity ratio***.

decision table Chart that lists the predicted values of possible parameters based on the varying probabilities of certain events and the varying values of the parameters should those events take place.

declining-balance depreciation Way of determining depreciation charges by multiplying the book value of a fixed asset at the beginning of a specified accounting period by a constant percentage (derived by taking into account the acquisition cost, depreciable life and scrap value of the asset). It is also termed reducing-balance depreciation.

declining-balance method *See* ***declining-balance depreciation***.

decommissioning cost Expense incurred by stopping an activity or operation (such as the cost of making good and landscaping the site of an open-cast mine).

deductions at source Income tax deducted by an employer from an employee's pay before he or she receives it, or the deduction of income tax from interest earned by, for example, a building society account. The sum deducted is then paid by the company to the Inland Revenue. Deductions at source help to prevent tax evasion.

deed of assignment *See* ***assignment***.

deep pocket Description of a company or person who seems to have plenty of money (and may therefore be worth suing). A deep-pocket view of some subsidiaries is that they may have access to more funds than an independent company of a similar size. A subsidiary may thus be able to call upon the greater resources of its parent company to engage in competition with independents in its sector.

defalcation Misappropriation of another's funds or property in one's care; embezzlement.

default Failure to comply with the terms set out in a contract. Legal proceedings generally follow if the matter cannot be settled amicably (*see* ***default notice***).

default notice Notice issued by a lender to a borrower who is in default of a loan subject to the Consumer Credit Act 1974. If the notice is not complied with, the lender can seek an ***enforcement order***.

D

defeasance Condition built into the wording of a deed that renders the deed void if the condition is complied with. The term is also used for any annulment or act that renders something null and void, such as the removal from a company's balance sheet liabilities that have no right to early repayment.

defective accounts Accounts that do not comply with proper accounting standards or with the law. If they are company accounts, revised accounts may be required under the terms of the Companies Act 1989.

defensive interval Ratio defined simply as quick assets divided by cash expenditure per day, i.e., how long a company can operate on its current assets. It is thus one measure of a company's liquidy and ability to meet current commitments without having to seek revenue elsewhere.

deferral method Method of spreading the befits accruing from an asset over the whole life of the asset, rather than accounting for it in the financial year of its acquisition. *See* ***deferred asset***.

deferred asset Also called deferred debit or deferred expense, expenditure incurred within a given accounting period but not balanced by the income it will produce, under the accruals concept. It is therefore regarded as an asset (not an operating cost), although it will become an operating cost when charged against any future income it generates.

deferred charge Outgoings that are not regarded as an expense in the accounting period in which they occur but which are carried forward (as an asset) and written off in a later accounting period. It is also known as a deferred cost.

deferred consideration agreement Agreement that payment of a consideration is to be put off, either until a particular event occurs or until a specified date.

deferred cost Alternative term for ***deferred charge***.

deferred credit Also known as deferred income, deferred liability or deferred revenue, income received before it is earned in a given accounting period, such as a government grant or an advance from a customer. In the USA, the term is also used for ***deferred income tax*** liability.

deferred debit Alternative term for ***deferred asset***.

deferred expense Alternative term for ***deferred asset***.

deferred income Alternative term for ***deferred credit***.

deferred income tax In US company accounting, a balance-sheet liability relating to additional federal income tax that would have been due if deducted expenses were not larger (in terms of tax) than actually recorded (in terms of financial reporting).

deferred liability Liability that does not fall due until after a period of a year. *See also* ***deferred credit***.

deferred revenue Alternative term for ***deferred credit***.

deferred taxation Tax for which a company or person is liable, but which has not yet been considered or demanded by the Inland Revenue.

deficit Excess of expenditure over income, or liabilities over assets; it is therefore a loss.

deflation Persistent decrease in prices, generally caused by a fall in the level of economic activity within a country; the opposite of inflation. It should not be confused with ***disinflation***.

delivery lead time Time that elapses between the placing of an order and its receipt, most often applied to stock ordering.

delivery note Document that advises a recipient of the intended delivery of goods or that accompanies goods on delivery.

demand deposit *See* ***time deposit***.

denominator variance Also termed production-volume variance, the budgeted fixed factory overhead less the fixed factory overhead as applied to units produced.

denominator volume Also termed production volume, the production capacity expressed as the ratio between the number of units expected and the budgeted fixed costs, thus giving the fixed costs per unit produced.

department Identifiable section of a company, often made a cost centre and assigned its own costs and credited with its own revenue.

departmental accounting Drawing up of accounts for each department of an organization, so that each can be regarded as a separate cost or profit centre.

departmental budget Budget drawn up for a specific department of an organization (for a specified period).

depletion Consumption of a natural resource or ***wasting asset*** (one that cannot be replaced, such as a mineral deposit).

depletion accounting Way of estimating the depreciation of a ***wasting asset***,

D

based on the rate at which it is being consumed.

depletion allowance Under US tax laws, a deductible expense calculated as a percentage of gross income from a wasting asset such as a natural resource (independently of the unamortized value of the asset). It is also called percentage depletion.

deposit Initial payment made on an item to reserve it, or an initial payment for something bought on credit or by hire purchase. The term is also used for goods or money placed with a bank or other financial institution.

deposits in transit Deposits made by a company (at a bank) that are not yet recorded on its bank statement. Consequently the company's bank reconciliation statement may have to be adjusted.

depreciable amount Value of a fixed asset that is used as a basis for calculating depreciation. It depends on whether ***straight-line depreciation*** or ***declining-balance depreciation*** is being used.

depreciable asset Fixed asset that is subject to ***depreciation***.

depreciable cost Proportion of the cost of an asset that is charged off over its life through ***depreciation***. It is generally the acquisition cost minus scrap value.

depreciable life Time period over which the ***depreciable cost*** of an asset is allocated. For some plant and machinery, it may be expressed as units of activity (such as the number of hours a machine has been running).

depreciated cost Also called depreciated value or net book value (NBV), the value of an asset on a company's books minus any depreciation since purchase or revaluation.

depreciation Positive decline in the real value of a tangible asset because of consumption, wear or obsolescence. The concept of depreciation is widely used for the purpose of writing off the cost of an asset against profit over an extended period (its ***depreciable life***), irrespective of the real value of the asset. Depreciation is charged against income or the profit and loss account, and there are various ways of calculating it. *See also* ***historical cost accounting***.

depreciation rate Rate at which ***depreciation*** occurs or is applied for accounting purposes. It is generally expressed as a percentage and its value depends on whether ***straight-line depreciation*** or ***declining-balance depreciation*** is being used.

depreciation reserve Alternative term for ***accumulated depreciation***.

deprival value Value a company places on an asset (which may be its economic value, net realizable value or replacement cost).

derecognition Removal of assets and liabilities from a balance sheet after they have been recorded in a company's financial statements.

detection risk In an audit, the risk that the auditor will not detect any errors or misstatements in a financial record. *See also* ***audit risk***.

development cost Expense incurred by a company in order to improve a process or product. It is usually written off immediately to the profit and loss account, unless the process or product will probably create future income (when the cost can be written off against that income when it accrues).

development gains tax Former tax charged in the UK on the proceeds of land sold for development. In 1976 it was replaced by the development land tax, which was itself abolished in 1985.

development land tax *See* ***development gains tax***.

development-state enterprise Business in the USA that uses all its resources in establishing itself, usually because no revenues have yet been received or sales have not yet begun.

different costs for different purposes Management accounting principle that a company's management will probably require different information (and therefore different costs) for all of its various activities.

differential analysis Analysis of ***incremental costs***, or analysis of the likely effect (on income and outgoings) of a particular management decision.

differential cost Another term for ***incremental cost***, or for a cost that changes because of a particular management decision.

differential income Also called differential revenue, income that changes because of a particular management decision.

differential pricing Practice that occurs whenever there are varying prices according to different circumstances. For example, a retailer may charge more for goods or services purchased using a credit card than for those paid for in cash (or offer a discount on cash sales). The retailer must in law display a sign that such differential pricing applies.

differential revenue Alternative term for ***differential income***.

differentiated marketing Method of selling that recognizes the special needs of some customers (such as left-handed people or diabetics).

dilution Reduction in the skill of a workforce overall as comparatively unskilled workers are recruited in response to a rise in demand for a given product or service.

diminishing-balance method *See* ***declining-balance depreciation***.

direct charge voucher (DCV) Document that details the purchases of materials and/or parts which can be charged directly to a process or product, without being stocked in the company's stores.

direct cost Also called variable cost, the cost of materials, items or activities (including labour) that are directly involved in the production of goods, and without which those goods could not be produced in the short term. The prime cost is the total of direct expenses, direct labour and direct materials.

direct costing Also called marginal costing or variable costing, method of allocating only variable manufacturing costs to a product; fixed manufacturing costs (including overheads) are regarded as period expenses chargeable immediately to revenue.

direct cost of sales Cost of goods sold, in terms of direct expenses, direct labour and direct materials only (i.e., excluding any overheads).

direct data entry Method of recording financial transactions directly onto a computer system. In a large organization, each section or department has its own computer terminal for this purpose.

direct expenses Expenses that may be attributed to one or another factor of production. They are included in ***direct costs***.

direct hour Hour spent within a company working on a process, product, service or cost unit. It is stated in units such as direct labour hours or machine hours.

direct labour Members of a company's workforce who are directly involved in the production of goods or services. For example, a welder is a member of the direct labour force whereas an estimator is not.

direct labour cost Cost of wages paid to members of a company's workforce who are directly invoved in production (***direct labour***). It is sometimes termed direct wages.

direct labour efficiency variance Difference between the actual labour time (taken for an activity) and the standard time allowed for it, valued at the direct standard labour rate per hour. It reflects how labour efficiency affects budgeted profit.

direct labour hour Hour spent by a worker directly involved in a process, product, service or cost unit within a company.

direct labour hour rate Rate of pay per hour paid to direct labour (*see direct labour hour*), or, in ***absorption costing***, the budgeted cost centre overheads divided by the budgeted direct labour hours.

direct labour rate of pay variance Difference between the actual rate per hour paid to direct labour for an activity and the standard rate allowed for it, for the actual hours worked. It reflects how differences in direct labour rates of pay affect budgeted profit.

direct labour total cost variance Combination of the ***direct labour efficiency variance*** and the ***direct labour rate of pay variance***, which can be stated as the product of the standard rate per hour and the number of actual hours worked, minus the actual labour cost.

direct materials Materials that directly become part of a company's product or cost unit.

direct materials cost Money spent on ***direct materials***.

direct materials inventory Also called direct materials stocks, a list of raw materials held in a company's store awaiting use in production.

direct materials price variance Comparison between the actual price paid for ***direct materials*** used in production and the standard purchase price of the materials used. It reflects the way in which differences in direct material prices affect budgeted profit.

direct materials stocks Alternative term for ***direct materials inventory***.

direct materials total cost variance Combination of the ***direct materials price variance*** and the ***direct materials usage variance***, which can be stated as the product of the standard price per unit of material and the actual units of material used, minus the actual materials cost.

direct materials usage variance Comparison between the actual amount of ***direct materials*** used in production and the standard quantity allowed, valued at the standard materials price per unit. It reflects how materials usage affects budgeted profit.

direct method Method of drawing up a cash-flow statement that aggregates operating cash receipts and payments to give the net cash flow from those operations.

director One of the principals of a company, in a public liability company (plc) appointed by its shareholders. Most companies have a group of directors (the board of directors) who act collectively as the senior management of the company, being responsible to the shareholders for its efficient running and future development. The duties and legal responsibilities of a director are defined in the Companies Acts. They include the compilation of an ***annual report*** and the recommendation of an annual dividend on shares.

directors' interests Interest in a company's debentures, shares and share options held by directors of the company, which must in law be disclosed.

directors' remuneration Also sometimes known as directors' emoluments, money received by directors by virtue of their office, including fees, salaries, perquisites and other profit. Certain benefits and expenses paid by the company may also be deemed to be remuneration. The total (although not necessarily individual) directors' remuneration appears in the company's annual financial report.

directors' report Report by a company's directors to its shareholders, which is published with the annual accounts and filed with the Register of Companies at Companies House.

directors' valuation Right of a board of directors to estimate the value of a company's shareholding in an unquoted company. The directors' valuation is called for only if the value of the shares concerned has changed since they were purchased.

direct posting Type of book-keeping in which there is no journal but entries are made directly into ledgers.

direct production cost of sales Alternative term for ***direct cost of sales***.

direct taxation System of taxation whereby companies and individuals pay tax on income directly the authorities (Inland Revenue in the UK, Internal Revenue Service in the USA) or through an employer, as opposed to indirect taxation, in which tax is added to the prices of goods and services.

direct wages Alternative term for ***direct labour cost***.

direct worker Company employee who spends so much of his or her time working on a product or cost unit that the employee's time can be assigned to the product as a ***direct cost***.

direct write-off method US method, obligatory for tax purposes, of writing off bad debts as they occur, rather than making a provision for them. It is not used for company financial reporting.

disbursement Payment made on behalf of a client by a banker, solicitor or other professional person. It is ultimately charged to the client's account.

disclaimer of opinion Auditor's report that states that he or she is unable to give an opinion on the financial statements being audited.

disclosure Revealing of pertinent information. For example, it is a requirement that a limited company must disclose its financial dealings and position by the publication of an annual report and accounts, and deposit them at Companies House along with a list of directors and shareholders in the company.

discontinued operations Profit and loss account should show separately the results of operations that have been sold or permanently closed down.

discount To make a reduction in the face value of an article (or the list price), generally in order to make the purchase more attractive to a customer or perhaps for paying by cash. Bulk discounts and trade discounts are also sometimes available. Discounts are shown as expenses in a company's profit and loss account. The term has several other meanings.

discounted bailout period US term for the time that must elapse before the net accumulated cash flow (from a project) is greater than or equal to the present value of net accumulated cash outflows. It is significant when budgeting capital expenditure on the project.

discounted cash flow (DCF) Method of assessing a company's investments according to when they are due to yield their expected returns, in order to indicate cash flows and the present worth of the future sum. In this way it is possible to determine preferences for one of a number of alternative investments.

discounted payback period US term for the time on a project during which the discounted present value of cash flows (inwards) equals the discounted present cash flows (outwards).

discounted value Also called present value, the product of projected annual cash flow and a discount factor determined by applying a ***hurdle rate*** of interest to the time period (*see* ***discount factor***).

D

discount factor Also called present-value factor, factor that, when applied to a predicted annual cash flow, converts it to a present value. It is equal to $1/(1 + r)^t$, where r is the ***hurdle rate*** and *t* is the duration of the project concerned.

discounting Act of making a ***discount*** or applying ***discount factors***. More specifically, it is the practice of selling a debt at a discount to an institution.

discounting back Method of estimating the present value of a future sum, carried out by finding what sum earning *x* per cent compound interest over the time in question will equal the future sum. The interest rate *x* is the one in use when the calculation is made.

discount lost Also called discount lapsed, the discount offered for prompt payment but not taken up in time by the purchaser.

discount rate Interest rate applied to future earnings to convert them to present values. It is the ***cost of capital*** rate of interest or ***hurdle rate*** used with a discount factor in calculating a ***discounted cash flow***.

discount received Discount given to a supplier, perhaps for cash payment or a bulk order. It is entered as a credit in the profit and loss account.

discovery-value accounting US method of accounting used in oil and gas extraction industries. It capitalizes the whole of the net realizable value of an extracted mineral, crediting it to income or contributed capital after deducting the exploration costs. *See also* ***dry-hole accounting***.

discretionary account (DA) Account into which ***discretionary funds*** are placed.

discretionary costs Also called managed costs, costs that result from a management decision (such as money spent on advertising or research).

discretionary funds Money left with a stockbroker, to be invested at his or her discretion.

discretionary grant Grant that is not automatically paid, but is made at the discretion of the authority concerned (as opposed to a mandatory grant).

discussion memorandum Document published by the US ***Financial Accounting Standards Board (FASB)*** before it publishes a Statement of Financial Accounting Standard.

disinflation Curbing of ***inflation*** by the adoption of mild economic measures such as the restriction of government expenditure. Other measures include increasing interest rates and the deliberate creation of a budget surplus. Disinflation is a mild form of ***deflation***, which by contrast indicates an uncontrolled fall in prices.

disintermediation Withdrawal of a financial intermediary from a negotiation. The term may also be applied to the flow of funds from lenders to borrowers 'off the balance sheet' without the intervention of an intermediary (such as a mortgage broker).

disposable income That part of a person's income that he or she may dispose of in any way, i.e., what is left after such necessities as accommodation and food have been paid for.

disposables Non-durable goods; those that are consumed during their use. Food, drink and fuel are all disposables.

disposals account Account detailing the disposal of a fixed asset. It consists of the original cost (which is debited), accumulated depreciation (credited) and price obtained (credited). The balance is the profit or loss on the transaction.

disposal value Also called net residual value or terminal value, amount that can be expected from the sale of an asset (less costs of sale). It is used in calculating ***depreciation*** and included in cash-flow predictions.

disproportionate expense and undue delay Reason why the consolidated financial accounts of a group of companies might exclude the figures for one of the subsidiaries (because it would cost too much and take too long to get them). It is not permitted if inclusion of the subsidiary would make a material difference to the accounts.

dissimilar activities Reason why the consolidated financial accounts of a group of companies might exclude the figures for one of the subsidiaries (because its activities are so different that their inclusion would give a distorted view of the group as a whole).

distributable income Also called distributable profits, the part of a company's net income that can be distributed to its owners (i.e., as dividends to its shareholders) without putting any strain on the company's finances or ability to continue in business. A public company must not allow its net assets to become less than the sum of its called-up share capital and undistributable reserves.

distributable profits Alternative term for ***distributable income***.

distributable reserves Retained profits that a company can distribute to its shareholders.

distribution cost Expense incurred by a company in advertising, selling and delivering goods, including the costs of packaging, insurance, and postage or transport. It is also known as distribution expense or distribution overhead.

distribution expense Alternative term for ***distribution cost***.

distribution overhead Alternative term for ***distribution cost***.

dividend A share in the profits of a limited company, usually paid annually. Dividends are usually expressed as a percentage of the nominal value of a single ordinary share. Thus a payment of 10p on each £1 share (or 10c on each $1 share) would be termed a dividend of 10%. They may also be expressed in terms of the dividend yield, which is the dividend expressed as a percentage of the share value. Dividends are determined by the directors of a company and are announced at the end of the annual general meeting (AGM) of the company.

dividend equalization account Method of stabilizing dividends of a company whose annual profit varies considerably (because of the nature of its business). Each year, funds are allocated to this reserve from the profit and loss account (more in some years than in others), and an average dividend paid based on profits averaged over several years.

dividend yield *See* ***dividend***.

dollar value LIFO In US accounting practice, a type of inventory (stock) accounting in which the stock quantities are expressed in dollars value, rather than in physical terms. Price changes are accommodated by applying an appropriate price index to the figures. *See also* ***last in first out (LIFO)***.

donated capital US term for an asset presented to a company as a gift. It is recorded in a donated-capital account as part of the shareholders' equity.

double account system Formerly used by private utilities and railway companies before privatization, an outmoded method of presenting financial statements.

double-declining-balance depreciation Method estimating ***depreciation*** by taking the historical cost or revalued worth of an asset, dividing it by its estimated life in years, and doubling the result.

double-entry book-keeping Method of recording financial transactions under two parallel headings, debits and credits, so that all accounts must balance (thus preserving the equality of the accounting equation).

double-entry cost accounting Keeping cost-accounting records using the methods of double-entry book-keeping.

double T-account Type of ***T-account*** in which an extra horizontal line is drawn to indicate a change in the account balance, which subsequent entries explain.

doubtful accounts US term for accounts receivable that are reckoned to be uncollectible. *See* ***bad debt; doubtful debts***.

doubtful debts Money that is owed but thought unlikely to be paid. Provision can be made for such sums in a company's accounts until they become ***bad debts***.

downstream Describing the movement of funds from a parent company to one of its subsidiaries.

dr Abbreviation of ***debtor***.

draft Written order from a customer to a financial institution, requesting that money is paid from the customer's account to a third party (such as a banker's draft). To draft is to draw up any document, especially a contract.

drawings Payments (or goods in kind) made to a partner or sole proprietor. *See* ***drawings account***.

drawings account Temporary account set up by partnerships or sole proprietorships in which are detailed payments to owners or partners. At the end of the accounting period, the account is credited and closed, and the owner's or partner's share of income or capital account is debited.

dry-hole accounting US method of accounting used in oil and gas extraction industries. Also called successful-efforts accounting, it capitalizes the fraction of the exploration cost attributable to the successful discovery, charging the remainder of the exploration costs as an expense. *See also* ***discovery-value accounting***.

dual aspect Also known as duality, the accounting principle that each financial event has an aspect that gives rise to a debit and an aspect that gives rise to a credit.

dual pricing Method of costing transfers (of goods or services) between divisions of a single organization in order to encourage interdivisional transactions. The buying division may be charged only the marginal cost while crediting the full cost to the selling division.

duality *See* ***dual aspect***.

due diligence Analysis of the financial status and prospects of company before it receives a major investment of capital. It is usually carried out by an independent accountant.

durables Goods that are not consumed by their use but which endure for a reasonable period of time. Some manufacturers of durables incorporate some form of obsolescence to ensure a continuity of demand. *See also* ***disposables***.

duty Broadly, any tax levied by a public authority, particularly that imposed on imports, exports and manufactured goods.

duty-free Describing goods on which no ***duty*** has to be paid. The practice of allowing people entering or leaving a country to purchase duty-free goods at ports and airports ended in the EU in June 1999.

duty-paid Authenticated statement attached to goods on which duty has been paid, to facilitate their passage through customs.

E

E & OE Abbreviation of ***errors and omissions excepted***.

earned income Income received in exchange for labour, rather than derived from investments (for UK tax purposes, the definition does, however, include some pension payments and state benefits).

earned surplus Former US term for ***retained earnings***. *See* ***surplus***.

earnings For a company, net income or profit (i.e., revenue minus expenses). *See also* ***earned income***.

earnings before interest and tax (EBIT) Company's profit, as shown on the profit and loss account, before deductions are made for tax and any interest owed.

earnings cycle Time during which a company coverts cash into goods or services, these goods or services are sold, and customers pay for them.

earnings yield Hypothetical figure that provides a reliable measurement of the worth of an investment. It is reached by relating a company's divisible net earnings to the market price of the investment (earnings per share divided by market price, expressed as a percentage). Sometimes, with reference to fixed-interest securities, the term is used interchangeably with ***flat yield***.

earn-out Employee incentive scheme whereby the employee is offered share options that give him or her an interest in the company for which he or she works. The term also describes an agreement to buy a company where the buyer pays a lump sum and promises to pay more if specified earnings levels are achieved. The latter is also known as a contingent agreement.

EBIT Abbreviation of ***earnings before interest and tax***.

economic appraisal Capital budgeting technique that employs ***discounted cash flows*** to evaluate a proposed investment or project.

economic benefit Estimated benefit that results from an ***economic appraisal*** of a proposed (usually government) project, such improvements to transport systems.

economic cost Total expense incurred in undertaking a certain activity, as predicted by an ***economic appraisal***. It includes accounting cost and opportunity cost.

economic income Income calculated by subtracting the net present value of future cash flows at the beginning of a period from the value at the end of the period.

economic life Time for which an asset can be expected to provide benefit. For some assets, such as a copyright or patent, it may be less than the actual legal life.

economic lot size Also called economic order quantity (EOQ), the quantity of inventory (stock) that should be ordered or produced at any one time to minimize the annual cost of holding stock.

economic order quantity (EOQ) Alternative term for ***economic lot size***.

economic profit In simple accounting, profit calculated as the difference between cost and income. In economics, however, economic profit also takes into account opportunity cost (*see* ***economic cost***).

economic value For an asset, the present value of future revenue it is expected to produce.

economies of scale Reduction in the average cost of production with increase in production, generally made possible by the large size of a company or industry. Internal economics of scale are defined as those enjoyed by a large single company or operation and are, broadly, made possible by the distribution of indirect costs and improvements in technology, which increase the optimum level of output. External economies of scale are those associated with an industry or location. For example, a concentration of ship-building companies on a river leads to the creation of a large pool of skilled labour which can be drawn on if one company wishes to expand.

ECU Abbreviation of ***European Currency Unit***.

effective annual rate Total interest earned or paid in one year stated as a percentage of the principal at the beginning of that year.

effective units Also called equivalent units, the units of production that are unfinished at the end of an accounting period and therefore designated work in progress. Each cost area is assigned a degree of completion in order to allocate a notional number for units effectively completed.

effective yield Yield calculated as a percentage of the price of an investment.

efficiency In general, a measure of the use of resources. High efficiency is achieved by getting the most output from the least input. In a manufacturing company, for example, efficiency can be measured in terms of the standard hours allowed for a certain amount of production and the actual hours taken to achieve it (known as the efficiency ratio).

efficiency ratio *See* ***efficiency***.

efficiency variance In standard costing, the quantity variance for direct labour or for a variable overhead. For direct labour, it is equal to the product of the standard rate per direct labour hour and the difference between the standard hours allowed for production and the actual hours taken. For variable overhead, it equals the product of the standard variable overhead absorption rate and the difference between the standard hours allowed for production and the actual hours taken.

efficient market hypothesis Assumption that market prices reflect all the information currently available and react virtually instantaneously to new information in an unbiased way.

eighth directive EC (as it then was) directive of 1984 concerning auditors and their regulation. In the UK, the provisions were incorporated into the Companies Act 1989.

EITF Abbreviation of ***Emerging Issues Task Force***.

elements of cost For any production process, the assignment of costs to expenses, labour and materials.

eliminations Entries made in the preparation of a consolidated account to ensure that assets, liabilities, and so on of the consolidated entity are not duplicated when adding together the accounts of the parent company and its subsidiaries.

embedded audit facility Program and data supplied by an auditor for incorporation into a company's computerized accounting system, thus allowing the auditor to make a continuous review of the company's financial status.

embezzlement Theft by an employee of money belonging to his or her employer.

Emerging Issues Task Force (EITF) In the USA, an organization of the Financial Accounting Standards Board (FASB) which indicates how new accounting problems and techniques should be dealt with (without having to wait for a Statement of Financial Accounting Standard to be prepared and published). *See also* ***Urgent Issues Task Force***.

emolument Salary and other benefits, particularly those paid the holder of high office. *See* ***directors' remuneration***.

emphasis of matter Former way in which an auditor drew attention to important elements in a company's financial statements. This option is no longer available to auditors in the UK.

employee report Report about a company's financial status issued by the board of directors to its employees. It is usually a simplified version of the official annual report and accounts.

employment costs Cost incurred in employing staff, including bonuses, incentives, salaries, wages and the employer's contributions to National Insurance and any pension scheme.

employment report Documentary account about a company's employees, included their numbers; names, ages and sex; costs of employing them; and health and safety measures in place. It may be appended to the company's annual report.

enabling cost Type of capacity cost that is incurred in full while operations continue (at any level) but which ceases if operations are completely shut down. An example is the cost of a quality control section.

encumbrance In US government accounting, an expected expenditure or funds set aside for such (for example, to pay for goods ordered but not yet delivered).

ending inventory Also called closing inventory, an inventory (list of stock and its value) at the end of an accounting period, as recorded in US accounting practice.

endorsee Person who receives the value of an order for payment (such as a cheque) that has been endorsed. *See* ***endorsement***.

endorsement Signature or explanatory statement on a document. For example, an open cheque cashed at a bank or transferred by the payee to a third party must bear the payee's endorsement on the reverse. The term is sometimes spelled indorsement.

endorser Person who signs an ***endorsement***.

enforcement order Court order that deals with a default on a loan subject to the Consumer Credit Act 1974. *See also* ***default notice***.

engagement letter Letter from an auditor detailing his or her responsibilities in a given engagement.

engineered cost Any cost that can be specifically related to a particular measure of activity. Using such costs, as estimated, for each stage in a production process, for example, managers can calculate the likely overall cost of the process. This can then be used in drawing up budgets and planning the requirements for staff and equipment.

enrolled agent Agent acknowledged by the US Treasury Department as being able to represent a taxpayer in his or her dealings with the Internal Revenue Serrvice.

enterprise fund Fund set up by a US government organization to account for services (generally utilities) that are self-supporting through charges made to their users.

entertainment allowance Amount an executive of a company is allowed to spend on entertaining clients or potential clients during the course of his or her business.

entertainment expenses Expense of entertaining business associates (for example, the cost of meals in restaurants or seats in a theatre).

entity In general in accounting, a particular focus of accountability. It can be almost anything from a local council, a company, a government department or a manufacturing process to an international corporation. A more strict definition is that an entity is any organization that has to prepare an annual report and accounts. This limits it mainly to corporate bodies, partnerships and sole proprietorships that carry on business in order to make a profit (although charities are also regarded as entities).

entity theory Also called the entity view, the idea that an accounting ***entity*** is an organization (in business to make a profit) and is separate from its owners (which are emphasized in ***proprietorship theory***). It is summed up by the accounting equation: assets = equities.

entity view Alternative term for ***entity theory***.

entry Item of information entered into a manual or computerized record, as in, for example, double-entry book-keeping.

entry value Current cost of buying an asset (at a fair market price); i.e., its replacement cost.

environmental accounting Also known as green reporting, method of including in a company's accounts attempts to detail the costs and benefits of the company's activities as they affect the environment.

environmental audit Also known as a green audit, an audit that reveals the impact of a company's activities on the environment.

EOQ Abbreviation of economic order quantity; *see* ***economic lot size***.

equal-instalment depreciation Alternative term for ***straight-line depreciation***.

equalization reserve US term for an allowance account for such items as the cost of maintaining plant and equipment (*see* ***accumulated depreciation***).

equipment trust certificate In the USA, a document that that details a loan raised to purchase a fixed asset. It gives the holder of the certificate a secured interest in the asset in case the borrower defaults on repayment of the loan.

equitable apportionment Method of fairly sharing common costs between two or more cost centres. *See* ***basis of apportionment***.

equity In general terms, the concept of fairness, of central importance to a branch of law distinct from common law, and as such having a significant effect on all kinds of contracts, dealings and trusts. The term also has various specific meanings. It is the ordinary share capital (risk capital) of a company, or a company's net assets, or the residual value of common stock over the debit balance of a margin account, or the difference between the market value of a property and the outstanding mortgage on it. In the last definition, if the amount still owing is greater than the present market value of the property, the mortgagor (borrower) has negative equity in the property.

equity accounting Stating in a company's accounts any share it holds in the undistributed profits of another company (in which it has an equity share).

equity capital Capital of a company that belongs to its owners (in many cases, holders of ordinary shares), rather than capital provided by owners of fixed-interest securities.

equity finance Funds raided by a company from its ordinary shareholders (as opposed to from debt finance and non-equity shares).

equity gearing Ratio of a company's borrowing to its equity.

equity method Method of accounting for long-term investments at cost plus a proportionate share of the retained income that has accumulated since their acquisition. In the USA, where it is sometimes called the soak-up method, it is used if a company owns more than 20% of the shares of another company. In the UK, the equity method is used in accounting for revenue from associates in which the investor has a financial interest.

equity share Any share that is a not a ***non-equity share***.

equity share capital *See* ***equity capital***.

equivalent production Also called equivalent units, the number of units of production that would incur the same costs as those that are actually incurred during an accounting period. It is useful when accounting for continuous production processes.

equivalent units Alternative term for ***effective units***. *See also* ***equivalent production***.

errors and omissions excepted (E & OE) Denial of responsibility for clerical errors and omissions, often included on invoices as a safeguard.

establishment charge Also called establishment fee, the overheads of a department store or shopping centre which are divided up and paid by the individual departments or shops. Establishment charges include rent, rates, taxes and the costs of heating and lighting.

estate duty Alternative term for ***death duty***.

estimated assessment In the UK, a tax assessment (made by the Inland Revenue) that is made on the estimated income or profits of an individual or corporate taxpayer. It is generally based on the revenue in the previous tax year, and is revised when the actual revenue is known. The practice of issuing estimated assessments to individuals largely ceased with the introduction of self-assessment.

estimated expenses *See* ***after cost***.

estimated liability Alternative term for estimated expenses (*see* ***after cost***).

estimated revenue In US government accounting, revenue that is expected during a particular accounting period, whether or not it is actual collected.

estimated salvage value Also called estimated scrap value, the ***scrap value*** of an asset while it is still in use.

ethical investment Investment made in a company that is not active in anything that the investor thinks is antisocial or unethical in its dealings. Thus some investors would not put money into companies that deal in or manufacture animal furs, armaments, cigarettes, and so on.

euro Standard currency unit of the European Monetary Union, introduced at the beginning of 1999 (but not adopted then by Denmark, Greece, Sweden and the UK). Until January 2002, only non-cash payments may be made in euros. *See also* ***European Currency Unit (ECU)***.

eurocurrency Currency of any nation held offshore in a European country. The eurocurrency markets deal in very large-scale loans and deposits rather than the purchase or sale of foreign exchange. *See also* ***euro***.

eurodollars US dollars held outside the USA, particularly those circulating in Europe. The postwar economic ascendancy of the USA has made the eurodollar an international currency medium. *See also* ***eurocurrency***.

European Currency Unit (ECU) Unit of account dating in use by the European Economic Union (EEC) from 1979 and now by the European Union (EU). The value of the ECU is calculated by taking a weighted average of the current value of EU member-states' own currencies. It exists on paper, but is used to settle intra-Union debts and in the calculation of Union budgets. Because it is an inherently stable currency, the ECU is increasingly favoured in the international money markets as a medium for international trade. *See also* ***euro***.

EV Abbreviation of ***expected value***.

event Any relevant occurrence that could happen, also sometimes known as a state of nature in the USA.

event of default In a loan agreement, a clause (such as a covenant) that if breached requires repayment of the loan immediately.

events accounting Accounting technique in which information is recorded and reported in terms of specified events, rather than chronologically, by value, or in any other manner.

ex ante Latin for 'from before' or 'before the event': what is expected to be the position after some future event. *See also* ***ex post***.

except for Also sometimes phrased 'with the exception of', a qualification in an auditor's report indicating that, although the financial statements audited give a true and fair view, some adjustments (approved by the auditor) may have been necessary. An example would be the change from one system of accounting to another.

exceptional and extraordinary items Significant below-the-line costs and revenues that arise outside the normal business activities of a quoted company. The sale or purchase of new buildings or plant might be examples of exceptional items.

excess capacity Capacity to produce goods over and above the current rate. Excess capacity is more strictly used to denote the increase in production necessary to bring the average production cost to a minimum.

excess material requisition Document completed by a company's production department to requisition materials required over and above the standard amount normally provided.

excess present value In capital budgeting, the anticipated net cash inflow less cash outflows, including initial outflow, for a process or product (stated in terms of present values).

excess profits tax Tax paid on a company's profit over and above a level that is thought to be normal. These profits result from economic conditions that favour the company but act against the majority of its competitors.

exchange Broadly, any transaction between one entity and another (formally, a reciprocal transfer).

Exchequer In its widest meaning, the central depository of UK government funds. As the department charged with the supervision of the nation's economic affairs, the Treasury is responsible for ensuring that all monies due to the government are paid to the Exchequer, and all spending approved by Parliament is paid for out of Exchequer funds.

excise duty Duty levied on home-produced goods, either to control consumption and thus influence spending, or to raise revenue. Goods that currently attract excise duty in the UK include alcohol, betting, petrol and tobacco. In the USA, a similar levy is known as excise tax.

excise tax *See* ***excise duty***.

executive director Also called a working director, a company director who is an employee of the company and therefore involved in its day-to-day management.

executory contract US term for a type of agreement that specifies payment on completion of some specified act. An example is a contract for providing labour for a project.

exempt private company From 1948, a family company that did not have to lodge financial statements with the Registrar of Companies. The

Companies Act 1967 abolished such status, which has since largely been replaced by the definitions of a ***small company*** and a ***medium-sized company***.

exempt supplies Good and services that are exempt from ***value added tax*** (VAT) in the UK.

exempt transfers Transfers of cash or property that are exempt from UK ***inheritance tax***.

ex-gratia Describing a payment made in thanks, such as a tip or golden handshake payment to a retiring employee. Most ex-gratia payments are tax free.

exit charge When an asset is removed from a discretionary trust, a charge made to inheritance tax.

exit value Price that would be obtained if an asset were sold in an arm's-length transaction; i.e., the ***net realizable value*** of an asset.

expendable fund In US government accounting, any fund whose earnings, principal and other resources can be distributed.

expectation gap In auditing, the difference between what auditors believe they have to do and what members of the public expect them to do.

expected deviations rate When an auditor performs a compliance test on a population (or sample), he or she expects to find some non-compliance with normal procedures; the expected deviations rate is the extent of this non-compliance.

expected error When an auditor performs a substantive test on a population (or sample), he or she expects to find some errors; the extent of these is the expected error.

expected value (EV) Arithmetic mean (average) of a statistical set of numbers or values. It may be expressed as the sum of the values and their probabilities.

expenditure At its simplest, any sum spent on attaining some object, such as cash paid for goods or services (assets). In accounting, acknowledgement of a liability is also an expenditure.

expenditure code Alternative term for ***account code***.

expenditure variance In standard costing, an overhead variance given by the difference between actual expenditure and budgeted expenditure.

expense account Sum of money that an employee can spend on out-of-pocket expenses (such as travel and entertainment) in order to do his or her job. In company accounting, the term also describes a ledger account in which the organization's costs are detailed under various expenditure headings. At the end of an accounting period, they are summed and transferred to the profit and loss account.

expenses Costs incurred by a company or individual in the course of normal activities, such as the value of assets consumed by a process (to produce goods or services).

expired costs Alternative term for ***expenses*** (in the company business sense).

explicit transactions Events that result in most day-to-day accounting entries, such as cash revenue or outgoings.

ex post Abbreviation of *ex post facto*, Latin for 'after the event'. It describes the position that arises after a certain event has taken place. *See also* ***ex ante***.

extended trial balance Type of ***trial balance*** that has three extra columns (for accruals, adjustments and prepayments) as well as additional columns for debits and credits as recorded in the profit and loss account.

external audit Independent audit of a company.

extraordinary item Non-recurrent material item listed below the line on a balance sheet, such as the sale or purchase of premises or a loss resulting from a major natural disaster, which would distort the profit and loss figures if not accounted for separately.

F

face value Also called nominal value, the price or value written on something, such as the denomination of a banknote or the par value of stocks or shares.

facility fee Alternative term for ***agency fee***.

factor Person or company that undertakes ***factoring.***

factoring Method of managing the trade debts of another organization. Commonly, a company sells due debts to a factor at a discount. The factor then makes a profit by recovering the debts at a price nearer the face value. Factoring relives companies of the burden of administering debts and gives them access to cash before payment is due.

factors of production Collective term for those things necessary for production to take place. They are usually divided into the following categories: capital, labour and land, to which may be added organizational ability (i.e., management).

factory burden US term for ***factory overhead***.

factory costs Costs of running the manufacturing wing of a company, including direct expenses, direct labour, direct materials and overheads allocated to production.

factory overhead Cost of running a manufacturing operation that cannot be directly allocated to the product (such as rent, maintenance and plant depreciation). It is also known as factory burden (USA), indirect manufacturing costs, manufacturing expense and manufacturing overhead.

fair copy Also known as a final copy, a copy of a document, including any alterations and revisions.

fair market price Price of an arm's-length transaction between a willing seller and a willing buyer, each acting in his or her own self-interest.

fair value Value of an asset that could be obtained in an arm's-length transaction between a willing seller and a willing buyer, each acting in his or her own self-interest.

FAPA Abbreviation of Fellow of the US Association of Public Accountants.

FASB Abbreviation of ***Financial Accounting Standards Board***.

favourable variance In standard costing, a situation in which actual revenues exceed budgeted revenues.

FCA Abbreviation of Fellow of the ***Institute of Chartered Accountants***.

FCT Abbreviation of Fellow of the ***Association of Corporate Treasurers***.

FIAB Abbreviation of Fellow of the ***International Association of Book-keepers***.

fictitious assets Assets that do not exist but which are entered into a company's balance sheet to balance the books. For example, a trading loss is a fictitious asset for purposes of taxation.

fiduciary Person or body acting in trust. Anybody holding, say, cash in trust for another is said to be acting in a fiduciary capacity.

filing of accounts Obligatory lodging of a UK company's financial statements with the Registrar of Companies at Companies House. *See also* ***abbreviated accounts***.

FIMBRA Abbreviation of ***Financial Intermediaries, Managers and Brokers Regulatory Association***.

final accounts Usually, a company's annual accounts. But the term may also refer to the final report submitted by a liquidator at the end of ***liquidation***.

finance In general, resources of money and their management, or to supply money (by whatever means) for a certain purpose.

Finance Act UK annual act of parliament that enforces the measures set out in the government's budget, particularly with respect to taxation for the coming year.

finance charge Sum charged for being able to delay payment of a debt until after the due date.

finance company Company that provides loans and other forms of finance.

finance house Company that provides funding (credit) for hire-purchase agreements. The finance house pays a trader in full, and charges interest to the purchaser of goods provided by the trader.

financial accountant Accountant who is concerned with the movement of cash, rather than with money that is involved in a company's production (*see* ***cost accountant***). The financial accountant is responsible for overseeing the level of cash available for paying debts and for investment, and for managing and recording all financial transactions.

financial accounting Branch of accounting that deals with the recording and classifying of a company's transactions, providing a true and fair view on the company's (annual) balance sheet.

Financial Accounting Foundation US organization that funds the activities of the ***Financial Accounting Standards Board (FASB)***.

Financial Accounting Standards Board (FASB) Private regulatory body, established in 1973, that sets the accounting standards for US public companies.

financial adaptability Ability of a company to change cash flows (both their amount and their timing) in response to the changes in need.

financial adviser Person (or institution) who gives advice on raising, lending or managing money, or on particular transactions, usually for a fee or commission. *See also* ***independent financial adviser (IFA)***.

financial analysis Analysis of a company's financial performance and status by referring to its financial statements.

Financial Analysts Federation International non-profit professional organization, established in 1947, whose members are financial analysts societies located in major cities of Canada and the USA. The total membership of these societies consists of financial analysts engaged in the profession of security analysis and investment management.

financial appraisal Choosing between alternative financial policies, usually by considering discounted cash flows and various ***financial ratios***.

financial asset Any asset that is cash or will yield or can be converted to cash.

financial budget Alternative name for ***cash budget***.

financial capital maintenance Amount of financial resources that have to be recovered before income begins; it excludes physical resources. *See also* ***capital maintenance concept***.

financial condition Alternative term for ***financial position***.

financial control Activities of a company's management that keep costs and revenue at acceptable levels. It is also termed financial management.

Financial Executives Institute US organization made up of chief accountants, controllers, treasurers and other financial executives of large companies.

financial expense Expense that is incurred in raising funds for a company or in managing them (such as interest on borrowing or senior executives' fees).

financial gearing *See* ***debt-equity ratio; gearing***.

financial highlights Summary of key financial data stated in a company's annual report and accounts. They may include such figures as dividends, profits and sales.

financial institution Finance house, bank, building society or any other institution that collects, invests and lends funds.

financial instrument Any method of financing, such as a bond, certificate of deposit (CD) or treasury bill.

Financial Intermediaries, Managers and Brokers Regulatory Association (FIMBRA) Former self-regulating organization that regulated financial advisers and a firms selling and managing securities and unit trusts. In 1994 its functions were incorporated into the ***Personal Investment Authority (PIA)***.

financial intermediary Finance house, insurance company, building society, bank or any other business that collects funds (from depositors or members) to use for making loans (to borrowers). Any person or organization that sells insurance (but is not an employee of an insurance company) is also regarded as a financial intermediary.

financial leverage *See* ***gearing***.

financial liability Obligation to pay (in cash or by means of another financial asset).

financial management Alternative term for ***financial control***.

financial period Period that elapses between the dates of two consecutive balance sheets (usually 12 months).

financial planning Working out short- and long-term strategies to determine financial targets for a company to aim for. Actual attainment can be measured against such planning.

financial position Also called financial condition, statement of a company's assets and equities, as detailed on the balance sheet. In general terms, the present condition of a person's finances is also sometimes called his or her financial position.

financial ratio Quantity used to assess the liquidity, profitability or solvency of a company, obtained by taking two appropriate figures from its financial statement and dividing one into the other, sometimes expressed as a percentage. There are many such ratios, such as acid-test ratio (quick ratio), all capital earnings rate, asset turnover, current ratio, days of average inventory in hand, debt-equity ratio, fixed-asset to equity-capital ratio, fixed-assets turnover, gross margin ratio, inventory turnover, price-earnings ratio, rate of return and receivables turnover, all of which have separate entries in this Dictionary.

financial report Also termed financial statement, an annual statement that sums up a company's activities over the previous year. It contains the balance sheet, profit and loss account, total gains and losses (statement of changes in financial position) and possibly cash-flow statements.

Financial Reporting Council (FRC) Organization that promotes good financial reporting, established in 1990 as a consequence of the ***Dearing Report***. It advises the ***Accounting Standards Board*** and appoints people to it.

Financial Reporting Exposure Draft (FRED) Discussion document issued by the ***Accounting Standards Board***, before it publishes a Financial Reporting Standard.

Financial Reporting Release (FRR) Announcement of policy by the US ***Securities and Exchange Commission***.

Financial Reporting Review Panel (FRRP) Group set up to examine the (defective) accounts of a company that has not followed required practice. It can get such accounts revised.

Financial Reporting Standard (FRS) Any of the standards (currently 15) issued since 1991 by the ***Accounting Standards Board***.

Financial Reporting Standard for smaller entities (FRSSE) Document issued by the ***Accounting Standards Board*** containing the requirements that apply to entities defined as ***small companies***.

Financial Services Act (FSA) 1986 Act of Parliament in the UK, in force since April 1988, introduced to prevent abuse of the de-regulated stock exchange system, principally by placing all people and institutions involved in financial services under the authority of a self-regulating organization (SRO). It implemented many of the recommendations of the ***Gower Report***.

financial statement Alternative term for ***financial report*** (of a company).

financial structure Alternative term for ***capital structure***.

financial year Period of twelve months, beginning at any time in the calendar year, used for company accounting purposes. Or, for purposes of corporation tax, it is the period of twelve months beginning on 1 April to which the tax applies. *See also* ***fiscal year***.

financing lease Also termed a capital lease, a lease that the lessee treats as both borrowing of funds and acquisition of an asset (to be amortized). The balance sheet recognizes both the asset and the liability.

finished goods Manufactured product that can immediately be sold.

finished goods inventory Also called finished goods stock, the value of manufactured product that can immediately be sold.

finished goods stock Alternative term for ***finished goods inventory***.

finished goods stocks budget Budget that accounts for the expected levels of finished goods held in stock at any time during the budget period.

firm Commonly, any company or business. Strictly, under UK law a firm is a partnership of professionally qualified people, such as accountants, civil engineers, lawyers or surveyors. In this case, the firms are legally distinct from companies and do not, for instance, issue shares. Also the liability of individual partners is not (and legally cannot be) limited.

firm offer Offer that has no conditions attached (and remains in force for a stated period).

first in first out (FIFO) Accountancy principle whereby stock-in-trade is assumed to be issued to customers in the order that it is received. Thus, stock currently held may be valued at current prices. *See also* ***last in first out (LIFO)***.

first-year allowance Capital allowance, rated at 40% between 2 July 1998 and 1 July 2000, that replaced the ***writing-down allowance***.

fiscal year Period of twelve months for the purposes of tax calculation. In the UK the fiscal year runs from 6 April to the following 5 April. In the USA, the term can be synonymous with ***financial year***.

fixed asset Also known as capital asset, an asset that is used in furtherance of a company's business, such as machinery or property. *See* ***capital asset***.

fixed-asset investment Money spent on tangible fixed assets that are expected to have a life of more than one year.

fixed-assets register Alternative term for ***assets register***.

fixed-asset to equity-capital ratio Value of a company's fixed assets divided by its equity capital. It gives an indication of the company's ability to cope with long-term debt.

fixed-assets turnover Sales revenue divided by the balance-sheet value of average total fixed assets. This ratio gives an indication of the company's activity during the accounting period.

fixed budget Budget that takes no account of any levels of activity that are different from those expected. It is also termed a static budget.

fixed capital Alternative tem for ***capital asset***.

fixed charge Part of the charge, usually made for a service, that is unchanged no matter how much a service is used. Examples of utilities that levy fixed charges are electricity, gas and some telephone companies. A fixed charge (also called a specific charge) is also a charge that gives a creditor the right to have an asset sold and the receipts put towards repayment of a debt that is outstanding. A legal mortgage is an example of such a fixed charge.

fixed cost Also called a fixed expense, a cost that does not vary with short-term changes in the level of output or sales (such as heating costs, business rates, and certain other overheads).

fixed expense Alternative term for ***fixed cost***.

fixed liability US term for a ***long-term liability***.

fixed manufacturing overhead applied In US accounting, the part of fixed manufacturing overhead costs that are allocated to units produced during the accounting period.

fixed overhead absorption rate Ratio of budgeted fixed overheads to budgeted standard hours or to units of budgeted production.

fixed overhead capacity variance Alternative term for ***capacity usage variance***.

fixed overhead cost Part of the indirect costs of a product that remains unchanged no matter how many units are produced or sold (such as the salaries of administrative and sales staff).

fixed overhead expenditure variance In standard costing, the difference between the budgeted fixed overhead and the actual fixed overhead incurred (for a given period).

fixed overhead total variance In standard costing, the difference between the fixed overhead absorbed and the actual fixed overhead incurred (for a given period).

fixed overhead volume variance In standard costing, the part of the fixed overhead total variance that indicates the degree of under-recovery or over-recovery of fixed overheads because actual activity differed from budgeted activity. It equals the recovered fixed overheads less the budgeted fixed overheads, and is also known as overhead volume variance.

fixed production overhead Part of factory overheads that remains unchanged no matter how many units are produced or sold (such as the salaries of factory managers and factory rent).

fixtures and fittings Immovable assets, fixed to land or property but not themselves part of the property.

flash report In the USA, a report by management highlighting things that need remedial action.

flat yield For a fixed-interest security, the true rate of interest defined in terms of actual income as a percentage of current purchase price (ignoring any benefit or penalty because of the nearness of the redemption date). It is sometimes called the ***earnings yield***.

flexed allowance For each of the variable costs items on a budget, their budget costs adjusted to reflect the actual level of activity.

flexed budget Budget adjusted to reflect actual levels of activity.

flexed budget allowance *See* ***flexed allowance***.

flexible budget Also termed variable budget, a budget that acknowledges that revenue and expenditure may vary from those budgeted for when the actual levels of activity are known.

flexible budget allowance *See* ***flexed allowance***.

flexible budget variance Alternative name for ***control budget variance***.

float Cash or funds used either to give change to customers or to pay for expenses (*see also* ***petty cash***). In the USA, cheques credited to someone's bank account but not yet debited to the drawer's account are also term float.

floating asset Alternative name for ***current asset***.

floating charge Charge over a company's assets that comes into effect only if a specified event occurs (such as liquidation of the company).

floor Fixed minimum interest for a loan; *see* ***collar***.

flow Change in the amount of something (such as stock) over time.

flow assumption Method of assigning cost to a withdrawal of stock (such as ***first in first out*** *or* ***last in first out***).

flow of costs Movement of costs through various activities within a company.

Flow of Funds Accounts National statistical system developed in the USA by the Federal Reserve Board and published regularly since 1947. It is constructed to show the financial activities of the US economy in a manner that enables financial activities to be related to the non-financial activities of the US economic functions that turn out income, savings, and goods and services.

footing US term for adding up a column of figures.

footnotes Additional detailed information appended to balance sheets and other financial statements.

forecast Estimated costs (outgoings), revenues (income), or both.

forecast reporting Incorporating projected figures (such as expected sales) in a company's financial report.

forensic accounting Accounting that involves, or is involved in, legal action.

Form 10-K In the USA, the Securities and Exchange Commission's (SEC's) annual report form, which a public company must file with the SEC within 90 days of its fiscal year-end.

Form 10-Q In the USA, the Securities and Exchange Commission's (SEC's) quarterly report form, on which a public company must detail interim financial statements (with comparative figures for the same period in the previous year).

Form 20-F In the USA, the Securities and Exchange Commission's (SEC's) annual report form which must be completed annually by non-USA companies.

format Company's (or its accountant's) chosen way of presenting financial statements which, in the case of balance sheets and profit and loss accounts, must comply with the requirements of the Companies Act.

formation expenses Cost of setting up a company, which have to be treated as one of its assets.

forward dating Dating a document (such as a cheque or invoice) in advance. Such a document is termed post-dated.

forward forward interest rate Rate of interest (for a deposit or loan) that begins on one future date and matures on a second future date.

forward integration Taking on by a company of activities at a subsequent stage of production or distribution (which could be carried out by another company). For example, an oil production company undertakes forward integration when it invests in refineries, tankers and petrol stations.

forward-rate agreement (FRA) Contract that states the rate of interest for a future deposit or loan, although this might not occur.

FRA Abbreviation of ***forward-rate agreement***.

franchise Licence bought by a retailer of goods or supplier of services that entitles him or her to sell the products of a particular manufacturer under a particular trading name. This system enables the manufacturer to have direct control over who sells the goods, and often gives the seller exclusive rights to sell those products in his or her area.

fraud Illegal practice of obtaining money from people under false pretences. For example, fraud is committed if facts pertaining to a contract are purposefully misrepresented. Fraudulently diverting one's company's or employer's money for one's own use is ***embezzlement***.

FRC Abbreviation of ***Financial Reporting Council***.

FRED Abbreviation of ***Financial Reporting Exposure Draft***.

free depreciation Depreciation of a company's asset over any time period it thinks fit.

free in and out Describing a selling price that includes the costs of loading and unloading the goods.

freight in Transport cost incurred in acquiring stock, accounted for as part of its cost.

freight out Transport cost incurred in selling stock, accounted for as a selling expense.

fringe benefit Item that is given to an employee as part of his or her payment but apart from wages or salary (such as a company car, health insurance, or goods at a discount). Fringe benefits are usually taxable.

front-end fee Non-returnable fee charged for borrowing money.

front-end loading Practice of including charges such as administrative costs and commission with the first repayment of a loan or the first payment of an insurance premium, with the result that the first payment is larger than the remainder.

frozen assets Assets that may not be converted into ready money without incurring a loss of some kind, or which may not be converted because someone has claim on them or there is an order that they may not be transferred. The latter is also called a frozen fund. *See also* ***liquid assets***.

FRR Abbreviation of ***Financial Reporting Release***.

FRRP Abbreviation of ***Financial Reporting Review Panel***.

FRS Abbreviation of ***Financial Reporting Standard***.

FRSSE Abbreviation of ***Financial Reporting Standard for smaller entities***.

FSA Abbreviation of ***Financial Services Act***.

full absorption costing Method of costing in which units produced bear the full costs of production (including overheads).

full consolidation Method of consolidation in which the consolidated accounts of a group include 100% of each item of all the wholly-owned subsidiaries' activities.

full costing Alternative US term for ***absorption costing***. In the UK it is usually taken to mean a costing method in which all of a company's costs (direct and overhead) are charged to a product or service (i.e., total absorption costing).

full cost pricing Way of fixing a product's selling price to make sure that it covers all the costs incurred in producing and supplying it.

full disclosure Principle that all material or significant information should be included in financial statements.

functional budget Budget drawn up to cover the activities of one of a company's functions (such as finance, production or sales).

functional classification Method of dealing with costs by assigning them to various functions within a company (such as administrative expenses, warehousing costs, cost of sales, and so on).

functional costing Costing in terms of a company's functions. *See* ***functional classification***.

functional currency For a company that does business in several countries, the currency of the country in which most business is done (which it usually employs in drawing up its accounts).

function costing *See* ***functional classification***.

fund Money or other asset set aside for a specific purpose, or lent to an institution or government. It is also any resource managed on behalf of a client by a financial institution.

fundamental accounting concepts Alternative term for ***accounting concepts***.

fundamental analysis Detailed analysis of a quoted company's annual report and accounts to check on the market value of its shares.

fundamental error Significant mistake in (or omission from) a company's accounts. A prior-period adjustment is made if it applies to an earlier accounting period.

fund balance In US government accounting, amount by which a fund's assets exceed its liabilities and reserves (equivalent to the owners' equity in a profit-making organization).

funded debt Generally, any short-term debt that has been converted into a long-term debt.

funding Substituting long-term debt for short-term liabilities.

funds General term for working capital (i.e., current assets less current liabilities). Sometimes the term is limited to mean cash or cash and liquid assets.

funds flow statement Financial statement that itemizes the differences between two consecutive balance sheets of a company. It is no longer required now that cash-flow statements are obligatory.

funds statement Informal US term for a ***statement of changes in financial position***.

G

GAAP Abbreviation of ***generally accepted accounting principles***.

GAAS Abbreviation of ***generally accepted auditing standards***.

gain Alternative term for profit.

galloping inflation Alternative term for ***hyperinflation***.

G & A Abbreviation of ***general and administrative expenses***.

gearing Proportion of long-term debt to equity finance on the balance sheet of a company. More specifically, it is the ratio of borrowed capital to total capital employed, expressed as a percentage (gearing ratio). It is sometimes known by the equivalent US term leverage.

general and administrative expenses (G & A) Administrative expenses plus operating costs.

General Commissioners Unpaid body of local people who hear appeals against assessments of capital gains tax, corporation tax and income tax and disputes concerning them. *See also* ***Special Commissioners***.

general debt In US government accounting, a government unit's debt that it can legally pay from general revenues.

general expenses Non-specific expenses incurred in the day-to-day running of a company or business. More specifically, they are operating costs other than ones that are assignable to such areas as administration, cost of sales, and so on.

general fund Assets and liabilities of a non-profit making organization that have not been set aside for a specific purpose.

general journal Record that details of a company's transactions (as journal entries) as they occur.

general ledger Record of all of a company's financial statement accounts.

generally accepted accounting principles (GAAP) In the USA, the broad concepts and detailed conventions, procedures and rules of accounting (and to which financial statements have to conform). In the UK, the term refers to ***accounting principles***. .

generally accepted auditing standards (GAAS) In the USA, the ten standards that refer to an auditor's professional qualities and how he or she should conduct an audit and draw up an auditor's report.

general partner Partner whose liabilities for the debts of the partnership are unlimited.

general partnership Formal partnership in which each partner shares equally in the running of the business (and each partner's liability is unlimited).

general price index Index that indicates the current purchasing power of money, such as the ***Retail Price Index*** in the UK and the ***Consumer Price Index*** in the USA.

general-purpose financial statements Annual report and accounts of a company.

general reserves Also called revenue reserves, company profits not distributed to its shareholders.

gifts inter vivos Gifts made during the giver's lifetime. Their position with regard to inheritance tax depends on their value, when they were given, and who receives them.

gifts with reservation of benefit Gifts in which the giver retains some benefit (such as dividends from shares given away, or rent-free living accommodation in a property that is given away).

GM Abbreviation of ***gross margin***.

going concern assumption Alternative term for ***continuity of operations***.

going concern concept One of the basic ***accounting concepts*** by which a business is assumed to be a going concern – that is, that it will continue in business for the foreseeable future (unless circumstances change dramatically). On company accounts, assets are shown at cost or cost less depreciation, and not at the ***break-up value.***

good output Perfect output from an intermediate or final process, the process costing having already allowed for abnormal loss and normal loss.

goods Physical items manufactured, sold or exchanged, from raw materials to finished products (as opposed to services, for which no physical items are transferred).

goods available for sale Beginning inventory (stock) plus all acquisitions of finished goods during a given accounting period.

goods in process Alternative term for ***work in progress***.

goods on approval Goods delivered to a customer for which payment is not required unless the customer is satisfied. If the customer is not satisfied in a stated period of time the goods are returned to the supplier. A retailer may hold goods on approval, and return them if they are not sold.

goods on assignment Method of trading goods in which they are sent to an agent on consignment. Although the agent has no title to the goods, he or she may sell them on to a buyer. If the goods are not sold, they are returned to their owner.

goods received note (GRN) Document filled in by someone who receives goods that have been ordered, confirming that the goods are as specified in the order.

goodwill Value of a business over and above the book value of its identifiable or physical assets. Or it is the amount paid on acquisition of a business over and above its current market valuation (including any stock). It can refer, for example, to the literal good will of the established customers of a retail business (shop or restaurant) whose benevolent habit (or custom) of using it can be quantified. It may be identified as an intangible fixed asset and amortized (to the profit and loss account) during its economic life, or written off to reserves.

goodwill write-off reserve Reserve account to which ***goodwill*** is written off.

Government Accounting Standards Board In the USA, organization that is responsible for the accounting standards of government departments.

Gower Report Report drawn up for the UK government in 1984 by Professor J. Gower. It dealt with the protection of people making investments, and most of its recommendations were included in the ***Financial Services Act 1986***.

grace and notice provision Provision in a loan contract that prevents the immediate default of a borrower who fails to make a payment of interest or repayment of capital on time (perhaps because of an administrative mistake).

Graham-Rudman Amendment Legislation, introduced in stages in the USA, aimed at amending the Constitution to make it unconstitutional for the government to run a budget deficit.

gratuity Payment made voluntarily in excess of statutory or contractual obligations, such as a tip in a restaurant or a bonus payment on retirement. Regular gratuities are often regarded as earnings for tax purposes.

green audit Another term for ***environmental audit***.

Greenbury Report Report issued in the UK in 1995 by a committee under the chairmanship of Sir Richard Greenbury. It dealt with recommendations about director's pay previously referred to in the ***Cadbury Report***. It emphasized that companies should have a remuneration committee made up of non-executive directors, that notice periods should not exceed a year, and that information about remuneration policy should be outlined in the company's annual report and accounts.

green reporting Alternative term for ***environmental accounting***.

grey market Any semi-legal market, usually for goods that are in short supply; it is one that keeps within the letter if not the spirit of the law. The term is most usually applied to the market dealing in any stock or share whose issue has been announced but which has not yet taken place. Traders therefore gamble on the eventual selling price of the issue when it comes onto the market. *See also* ***black market***.

GRN Abbreviation of ***goods received note***.

gross Amount calculated before the deduction of certain items, the items generally being specified according to context. For example, a salary or interest paid 'gross of tax' is paid before deduction of income tax, in contrast to 'net of tax', where tax is deducted before payment.

gross annual value *See* ***annual value***.

gross book value Value of an asset before the deduction of any related expenses (such as depreciation).

gross corporation tax Total corporation tax due on a company's profits that are chargeable to this tax, before deductions of any ***advance corporation tax*** or income tax.

gross earnings Earnings before deduction of income tax (*see* **gross**).

grossing up Calculation of a gross amount from the net amount by adding back the amount deducted.

gross interest Interest on a deposit or investment before deduction of income tax (*see* **gross**).

gross margin (GM) Also called gross profit or gross profit margin, the price at which goods are sold minus what they cost, usually expressed as a percentage of the selling price. More formally it is the difference between a company's sales revenue and the cost of the goods sold, ignoring costs of administration, distribution or finance.

gross margin ratio Gross margin expressed as a percentage of sales, regarded as a measure of the success of a retail company. It is also called gross profit ratio.

gross mark-up Amount by which a trader increases the purchase price of an item in order to sell it at a profit, usually expressed as a percentage of its purchase price.

gross price method Accounting method in which a purchase or sale is recorded at its invoice price, ignoring any discount, which is noted in a contra account.

gross profit Alternative term for ***gross margin***.

gross profit method Method of determining ***ending inventory*** in US accounting practice by measuring the cost of goods sold as a fraction of sales and applying the ***inventory equation***.

gross profit percentage Alternative term for ***gross margin ratio***.

gross profit ratio Alternative term for ***gross margin ratio***.

gross sales Value of sales at invoice prices, without deduction of such things as allowances, discounts, returns, and so on. It is similar to the ***gross price method***.

gross up *See* ***grossing up***.

gross yield Return on an investment calculated before tax is deducted.

group accounts Alternative term for ***consolidated accounts***.

group depreciation Calculation of depreciation by combining similar assets, rather than by depreciating them individually.

group financial statements Alternative name for ***consolidated accounts***.

group income Dividend paid by one member of a group of companies to another member of the group. It is exempt from ***advance corporation tax***.

group relief Relief from corporation tax available to a group of companies by offsetting certain losses of one member of the group against the profit of another member (which must be 75% owned).

growth rate Change in the financial status of a company over a period of time, usually expressed as a percentage of profits or revenue.

guarantee Promise to pay the debt of somebody else in the event that the debtor defaults (compare with ***indemnity***). Guarantee is also the name given to a document stating that goods or services are of good (merchandizable) quality.

guarantor Person who guarantees, if necessary, to pay someone else's debt.

H

half-year convention US accounting practice of regarding depreciable assets acquired at any time during a year as being put into service half-way through the year.

Hampel Committee UK committee, chaired by Sir Ronald Hampel, that reviewed the implementation of the ***Cadbury Report*** and ***Greenbury Report*** and published its own report in 1998. It underlined the principle that company directors' main duty is to the company's shareholders.

hard currency Currency, widely used in international trade, from a country with a stable and prosperous economy. It is thus in high demand and preferred to less stable or legally restricted currencies.

harmonization Aim of bringing common principles and standards to financial reporting worldwide and particularly within the EU.

harvesting strategy Taking short-term profits from products just before they are withdrawn from the market (usually by reducing the spend on advertising).

haulage Cost of road transport. There may be additional charges for loading and unloading.

hidden price increase Decline in the real value of a good or service occasioned by a decrease in its quality or quantity rather than by a rise in its price.

hidden reserve Also called secret reserve, a reserve that is not declared on a company's balance sheet.

hidden tax Tax included in the price of goods so that it is not obvious to the consumer. Most forms of indirect taxation are hidden in this way, for example tax (duty) on alcohol, petrol and tobacco.

high-end Description of goods that are produced for the top of the market and are consequently very expensive.

higher-rate tax Rate of income tax that is higher than the ***basic rate***. It is currently set at 40% and for 1999-2000 was payable on taxable income of £28,001 and above (after allowances).

highlights Significant items emphasized in a company's annual report and accounts, usually relating to revenue, profits and dividends. *See also **flash report***.

high-low method Method of predicting costs according to activity level achieved by charting the costs at lowest and highest levels of activity and drawing a straight line between them. The resulting graph gives an indication of costs at intermediate activity levels.

hire purchase (HP) Form of credit, normally extended on consumer goods, in which the customer takes and uses the goods and pays for them in instalments (with interest) over an agreed period of time. The seller can in theory repossess the goods at any time if the hirer defaults on payment (unlike with a ***credit sale***). The finance for such business usually comes from a ***finance house***.

historical cost Cost of an asset at the time it was acquired, rather than the current cost of its replacement. It is also celled acquisition cost or original cost; some US accountants prefer the term ***sunk cost***.

historical cost accounting Method of assigning value to, for example, assets for accounting purposes. In historical cost accounting, the original cost of an asset is taken into account, rather than the cost of its replacement. It contrasts with ***current cost accounting***.

historical cost convention Convention in which assets are accounted for at their ***historical cost***.

historical summary Summary of financial results of the previous five years, as included in some company's annual accounts.

hive off To split off an operating arm of a company to make it into a subsidiary company. It is said to have hived off that part of its operation.

holding company Company that exists to hold shares in other companies, which are (depending on the level of shareholding) its subsidiaries. An immediate holding company is one that holds a controlling interest in another company but, in turn, the immediate holding company itself may be owned by a holding company. It is also known as a parent company.

holding gain Gain that accrues because of how long an asset has been held (rather than from its use in business activities). It is not realized until the asset is sold.

honararium Money paid to a professional such as an accountant or a solicitor when he or she does not request a fee.

horizontal form Method of presenting a financial statement with credits on one side (usually the left-hand side) and debts on the other (usually the right-hand side).

horizontal diversification Diversification into industries or businesses at the same stage of production as the diversifying company. For example, a suit manufacturer might diversify into leisurewear, or a yacht builder into the construction of motor boats. *See also* ***vertical diversification***.

horizontal integration Amalgamation of companies in the same stage of production, and which are therefore likely to possess similar skills and benefit from economies of scale.

HP Abbreviation of ***hire purchase***.

human capital Value of a company's employees.

human-resource accounting Method of recognizing and quantifying a company's human resources, and accounting for them in the company's accounts. The quantifying aspect has proved to be problematic.

hurdle rate In capital budgeting, the rate of interest that a proposal must exceed before it is given consideration; i.e., the required rate of return. It is usually related to the cost of capital, taking into account any risk factors.

hyperinflation Inflation (a general increase in price levels) that is running extremely high, also known as galloping inflation.

I

IAB Abbreviation of ***International Association of Book-keepers***.

IAS Abbreviation of ***International Accounting Standards*** and ***Institute of Accounting Staff***.

IASC Abbreviation of ***International Accounting Standards Committee***.

IAPC Abbreviation of ***International Auditing Practices Committee***.

ICAEW Abbreviation of ***Institute of Chartered Accountants in England and Wales***.

ICAI Abbreviation of ***Institute of Chartered Accountants in Ireland***.

ICAS Abbreviation of ***Institute of Chartered Accountants in Scotland***.

ICSA Abbreviation of ***Institute of Chartered Secretaries and Administrators***.

ICQ Abbreviation of ***internal control questionnaire***.

ideal capacity Minimum number of units that could be produced by a specific operation, neglecting stoppages through industrial action or for repairs.

ideal standard costs In standard costing, the standard costs that would be incurred in the best possible operating circumstances.

identifiable assets and liabilities Company's assets and liabilities that could be got rid of without disposing of the whole company.

idle capacity Unused part of a company's budgeted capacity, expressed in labour hours or machine hours.

idle capacity ratio Idle production capacity divided by budgeted capacity, often expressed as a percentage.

idle capacity variance Alternative term for ***capacity usage variance***.

idle time Time for which a production process cannot operate, measured in labour hours or machine hours. It usually requires wages to be paid to workers who are idle through no fault of their own.

IFA Abbreviation of ***independent financial adviser***.

IFAC Abbreviation of ***International Federation of Accountants***.

IHT Abbreviation of ***inheritance tax***.

IIA Abbreviation of ***Institute of Internal Auditors***.

illiquid Describing a company that has insufficient cash (or liquid assets) to pay its debts.

IMA Abbreviation of ***Institute of Management Accountants***.

immediate holding company *See* ***holding company***.

impairment For a fixed asset (or goodwill), a reduction in its recoverable amount below its ***carrying amount***.

impersonal accounts On a book-keeping ledger, an account that deals with capital and assets (the ***real accounts***) or income and expenditure (the ***nominal accounts***), or a combination of the two. The only element of the ledger the impersonal accounts do not cover is the record or creditors and debtors (the ***personal accounts***).

implicit transaction Event that is temporarily ignored in record keeping from day to day and is not subject to any adjustments at the end of the accounting period.

implied terms Terms of a contract that are not expressly stated, but that the law considers to be necessary to the sense of the contract and therefore implicit.

imprest fund Alternative name for a ***petty cash*** fund.

improvement Expenditure that improves the performance of or extends the useful life of an asset. It is capitalized as a proportion of the cost of the asset.

imputation system UK taxation system, established in 1973, which partly governs the payment of corporation tax. Under this system, a shareholder's dividends are taxed at source, and he or she is issued with a credit for the tax imputed.

imputed cost Cost that, although it does not actually exist, is included in accounting records in order to be able to compare costs with another operation that does incur such a cost.

income Money, goods or services received from an activity. Income may be a return on one of the factors of production – a salary, rent, interest or profit – or it may be a transfer payment made for other reasons, such as (in the UK) unemployment benefit. The definition also includes non-monetary income, such as the benefit a company or individual derives from the possession of assets. For a company it is therefore the amount by which revenue and gains exceed expenses and liabilities (debts).

income and expenditure account Similar in form to a profit and loss account, an income and expenditure account records all cash transactions over a given period. It is usally the form preferred by an organization whose primary aim is not to make a profit (such as a registered charity).

income bracket Range of incomes (salaries, wages), normally rated from a specific minimum to a specific maximum. The term also applies to people who are in that income range.

income code Alternative term for ***account code***.

income distribution account Temporary account that may be debited when a company declares its dividends.

income from continuing operations All of a company's revenues less all of its expenses, except for: gains or losses accrued on disposal of sectors of the company; gains or losses from extraordinary items; the results of operations that will be discontinued; and any effect of accounting changes.

income from discontinued operations Company's income from those parts of its activities that have been discontinued during the relevant accounting period.

income generating unit Collection of assets, liabilities and their associated goodwill that generate income independently of other strands of income.

income percentage of revenue Ratio of income to revenue expressed as a percentage.

income smoothing Type of ***creative accounting*** by means of which a company presents its financial figures in such a way as to eliminate large changes in profit, so appearing to have made smooth progress over the years (in order to give confidence to investors).

income standard In standard costing, the income level that selling a company's products is expected to achieve.

income statement US term for a ***profit and loss account***.

income tax Direct annual tax levied on ***income***, such as on fees, salaries and wages. In accounting terms it is regarded as an expense or, if not yet paid, a liability. *See* ***basic rate; higher-rate tax; standard rate***.

incomplete records Accounting records with some missing details (such as a partial record or one that has been omitted altogether). The missing items may have to be deuced from other documents on file.

incorporation Process of setting up a business as a legal entity.

incorporation of audit firms Method by which partners in a firm of auditors limit their liability in claims for negligence. The firm forms a limited company, owned by the partners, who nevertheless may, as individuals, be sued for damages.

increment Amount of an increase.

incremental Describing an upward change in something (such as cash flow, cost, investment, profit or revenue) that accompanies changes in production, sales, and so on.

incremental approach Analysis used to make decisions. Changes in costs that would occur if a certain decision is made are estimated and used to judge whether or not it is a good decision.

incremental budget Fairly unreliable method of preparing a budget by adding incremental amounts to the previous budget.

incremental cost Extra cost incurred when a company agrees to a certain course of action, such as taking on a new project, also called a relevant cost.

incremental increase Increase that occurs in steps or stages, or successive increases by one unit.

indebtedness State of owing money or services to someone else, or the amount of money owed.

indemnity Undertaking that gives protection against loss or damage. It may be in the form of replacement or repair of property lost or damaged, or the provision of cash to the value of the property.

independence Impartiality required of auditors, who should have no personal or financial involvement with any organization whose accounts they are auditing.

independence of auditors *See* ***independence***.

independent accountant Accountant who carries out the ***attest*** function for a company.

independent company Company that operates entirely under its own authority, and is not owned or controlled (in part or in whole) by any other company.

independent financial adviser (IFA) Financial adviser who can give advice about the products of any company (i.e., he or she is not tied to only one company as its employee or agent). He or she must offer best advice based on all the products available.

independent taxation Situation pertaining in the UK whereby a married woman is taxed separately from her husband (before 1990, a couple's joint income was taxed as if it were a single income).

index Form of measurement or comparison, or a listing that gives an indication of change. *See **index number**.*

indexation Form of index-linking that ties, say, income to the retail price index and therefore prevents a fall in real wages during a period of inflation. Annuities, pensions or taxes may also be index-linked. The term also describes an adjustment (the indexation allowance) to the value of an asset to take into account a change in the retail price index. This prevents the owner of the asset from having to pay capital gains tax on a gain that was due entirely to inflation.

indexation allowance *See **indexation**.*

index-linked *See **indexation**.*

index number Weighted average that permits the comparison of prices or production over a number of years. The components elected for comparison are weighted according to their importance and then averaged. Figures are compared to those for a base year, selected for its typicality and given the index number 100 or 1000.

indirect cost centre Also called service cost centre, service department or support cost, in absorption costing a cost centre to which the costs of non-production activities (such as stores and works' canteens) are allocated.

indirect costs Also called indirect expenses, costs of items or activities, such as maintenance of buildings or machinery, that are not used in the production of goods, nor are they immediately necessary for their production. They are generally regarded as overheads, although in some methods of costing they may be allocated to cost centres.

indirect expenses Alternative term for ***indirect costs***.

indirect labour Workers who are not directly involved in a production process (such as cleaners, maintenance staff and supervisors). In other words, all labour that is not ***direct labour***.

indirect labour costs Money paid to ***indirect labour***.

indirect manufacturing costs All manufacturing costs that are not direct labour costs or direct material costs.

indirect materials Materials that are not included in a final product but which are necessary for its production (such as cleansers and lubricants).

indirect materials cost Cost of providing ***indirect materials***.

indirect method In a cash-flow statement, method of adjusting the operating profit for non-cash credits and charges (so that it can be reconciled with the net cash flow from the operation).

indirect production Production of goods for sale by employing labour and machinery and using a system of divided labour in order to make a profit.

indirect taxation Tax paid to one person or organization (often a retailer), who then pays it to the Inland Revenue or Treasury. Duty and value added tax are forms of indirect taxation.

individual retirement account (IRA) The US Tax Reform Act 1976 authorized a qualified retirement plan for individuals.

industry segment Separate part of a company that produces a separate product or service.

inertia selling Method of selling in which unsolicited goods are mailed to a 'customer' and followed by an invoice. It is illegal in many countries.

inflation Persistent general increase in the level of prices. Strictly defined, it includes neither one-off increases in price (occasioned by, for example, a sudden scarcity of one product) nor any other increases caused by real factors. Its causes include an excess of demand over supply and increases in the money supply, perhaps brought about by increased government expenditure, which causes a decline in the real value of money.

inflation accounting Alternative term for ***current cost accounting***.

inflation-adjusted Describing wages that have been modified to maintain real income by increasing pay in line with inflation. The term may also be applied to the economist's technique of discounting price changes to obtain a truer picture of quantitative changes in output.

inflation tax Extra revenue accruing to the government because inflation has brought new taxpayers on stream or pushed taxpayers or taxable items into higher brackets.

inherent goodwill Goodwill that an existing business is assumed to have, not to be recorded on its balance sheet.

inheritance tax (IHT) Tax paid on inheritances by heirs, often calculated in relation to the closeness of the relationship between the heir and the deceased person. In the UK, capital gains tax covers income from inheritances.

initial allowance Amount deducted from a company's profits for the purposes of calculating tax in the first year after acquisition or setting up in business.

initial yield Ratio of an asset's gross initial annual income and its initial cost.

Inland Revenue UK government department whose major responsibility is the collection of various taxes, such as income tax, capital gains tax and corporation tax. Its full name is the Board of the Inland Revenue.

input tax In the UK value added tax system, the tax that is collected from the seller of goods by the Customs and Excise. *See also* ***output tax***.

insolvency State in which total liabilities (excluding equity capital) exceed total assets; it is therefore the inability to pay debts when called to do so. If insolvency is chronic, bankruptcy or liquidation generally follow.

insolvent Describing a person or company that is in a state of insolvency.

inspector general US federal office that audits federal agencies, periodically reporting to Congress.

Inspector of Taxes UK civil servant who works for the Inland Revenue, issuing assessments and tax returns, agreeing taxpayers' tax liabilities and conducting appeals.

instability index of earnings Measure of the reliability of a company's profitability, equal to the difference between actual profits and trend (expected) profit.

instalment Part payment of a debt, such as one undertaken as part of a ***credit sale*** or ***hire purchase*** agreement. Instalment payments fall due at fixed and specified intervals and when totalled equal the original debt, usually with the addition of interest.

instalment sales method US practice of accounting for gross margin (or revenues and expenses) from sales in proportion to the part of the selling price actually collected in a given accounting period.

Institute of Accounting Staff (IAS) Organization established in 1974 to represent accountants employed in industry or by accounting firms.

Institute of Certified Public Accountants Organization established in 1903 and, in 1932, amalgamated with the Central Association of Accountants. Then in 1941 this organization amalgamated with the Chartered Association of Certified Accountants.

Institute of Chartered Accountants Professional organization of chartered accountants in the UK, divided into the ***Institute of Chartered Accountants in England and Wales***, the ***Institute of Chartered Accountants in Ireland*** and the ***Institute of Chartered Accountants in Scotland***. These bodies set educational standards and coordinate training, set examinations and oversee the practice of accountancy in the UK.

Institute of Chartered Accountants in England and Wales (ICAEW) Organization established in 1880 by combining the Incorporated Society of Liverpool Accountants (founded in 1870), the Institute of Accountants in London (1870), the Manchester Institute of Accountants (1871), the Sheffield Institute of Accountants (1877) and the Society of Accountants in England (1871). In 1957 it amalgamated with the Society of Incorporated Accountants and Auditors, which had been founded in 1885.

Institute of Chartered Accountants in Ireland (ICAI) Organization, established in 1888, that represents accountants throughout Ireland (Northern Ireland and the Republic).

Institute of Chartered Accountants in Scotland (ICAS) Organization formed in 1951 by the amalgamation of the Aberdeen Society of Accountants (founded in 1867), the Edinburgh Society of Accountants (1854) and the Glasgow Institute of Accountants and Actuaries (1854).

Institute of Chartered Secretaries and Administrators (ICSA) Organization established in 1891 to represent company secretaries and administrators.

Institute of Internal Auditors (IIA) Organization established in 1945 to represent US accountants engaged in carrying out internal audits. It founded a branch in the UK in 1948.

Institute of Management Accountants (IMA) Organization originally established in the USA in 1919 as the National Association of Cost Accountants.

in-store concession In order to diversify yet maintain their own profits, some large stores allow smaller retail operations to set up and staff areas within the store for the sale of their own goods. The store then receives a percentage of the in-store concession's takings in payment.

instrument Broadly, any legally binding document (such as a ***financial instrument***).

intangible asset Non-monetary asset that is neither physical nor current. The many examples include brand names, copyright, ***franchises***, ***goodwill***, leases, licences, mailing lists, patents and ***trademarks***. It is sometimes known as an invisible asset.

intangible property Property with no physical actuality but which gives its owner a benefit (such as a trademark). *See also* ***intangible asset***.

integrated accounts Financial records in one set of books containing a company's cost accounts and financial accounts together (so that reconciliation of two different sets of books becomes unnecessary).

integrated test facility (ITF) Computerized auditing process, supplied by an auditor and incorporated into a company's computerized accounting system. It enables an auditor to enter, for example, details of a fictitious customer and check the 'transactions' through the system. A continuous check on processing functions can also be made.

Inter-American Accounting Association Organization which meets every two or three years to review the technical side of accounting in American countries.

interest Charge made by a lender to a borrower in exchange for the service of lending funds. It is usually expressed as a percentage of the sum borrowed for a specific period (normally a year), termed the interest rate, but it may be paid in kind. Interest is also payment made by a bank or building society to customers who deposit money with them. *See* ***compound interest; simple interest***.

interest cover Ratio of earnings to the fixed-interest payments necessary to service loan capital. It is an indication of how vulnerable a company is to fluctuations in profit or interest rates.

interest factor Interest rate plus one.

interest rate Interest charged to a borrower or paid to an investor, usually expressed as a percentage per annum (*see* ***interest***).

interest-rate risk Risk that variation in interest rates may affect the value of an asset or liability during its lifetime.

interest receivable account Ledger account in which interest receivable is recorded, to be later credited to the profit and loss account.

interest warrant Government cheque issued by the Bank of England for paying interest due on a loan. A company may also issue an interest warrant.

interim accounts Also called interim financial statements, short financial statements produced by a company (often unaudited) in the middle of the financial year halfway between publications of annual accounts. It is a requirement that listed companies produce such a half-yearly report.

interim financial statements Alternative name for ***interim accounts***.

interlocking accounts System that keeps cost accounts and financial accounts separate, using control accounts to reconcile them.

intermediate holding company Company that fulfils the functions of a ***holding company*** of one group of subsidiaries and is at the same time itself a subsidiary of a larger group.

intermediary Someone who acts between and deals with two parties who themselves make no direct contact with each other.

internal audit Audit of a company's books that takes place virtually continuously and is undertaken by internal staff, rather than by an external auditor. Internal auditing is carried out in order to monitor company profitability and guard against fraud.

internal auditor Auditor who belongs to a company's ***internal audit*** department.

internal check System of accounting that ensures that each person's work and financial dealings are checked by an independent third party within the company. Together with ***internal control***, it is a combination of self-regulatory measures by means of which a company ensures that each employee is accountable, safeguards its assets and institutes an accurate system of accounting, therefore enhancing its own efficiency.

internal control Methods used by an organization to minimize the risks of fraud, theft or false accounting, which are checked during an ***internal audit***. They include passwords, security measures (locks on stores, computer passwords, encryption), division of certain tasks between two or more people, and requiring two or more signatures on certain documents.

internal control questionnaire (ICQ) Document an auditor employs to check a company's ***internal control*** system. The answers allow auditors to devise substantive tests to detect errors.

internal control risk Risk that a company's ***internal control*** system will fail to prevent or detect errors.

internal control system *See **internal control**.*

internal rate of return (IRR) Discount rate at which, applied to the expected pattern of cash expenditure and income of a capital project, would give a net present value of zero. It may be compared with the return on alternative investments, or on some target rate of return.

Internal Revenue Code US federal tax law, as it applies to taxpayers.

Internal Revenue Service (IRS) US equivalent of the UK's ***Inland Revenue***.

internal accounting control *See **internal check**.*

International Accounting Standards (IAS) Standards published by the ***International Accounting Standards Committee***, in an attempt to make financial statements from different countries more compatible.

International Accounting Standards Committee (IASC) Organization established in 1973 to promote accounting standards worldwide. It has 95 members from throughout the world.

International Association of Book-keepers (IAB) Professional book-keepers' organization.

International Auditing Practices Committee (IAPC) Committee of the ***International Federation of Accountants*** which issues International Standards on Auditing (ISA) and publishes guidelines and exposure drafts on auditing practices.

International Federation of Accountants (IFAC) Organization established in 1977 to promote harmonized standards for accountancy throughout the world. Accounting organizations from 80 countries are members.

International Organization for Securities Commissions (IOSCO) Organization established in 1987 to establish international standards, particularly in respect of shares of multinational companies.

International Standards on Auditing (ISA) Standards published by the ***International Auditing Practices Committee***, which do not take precedence over local standards.

interpolation Estimating a quantity by locating it between two members of series of known quantities.

intervention price Price slightly below the ***threshold price*** at which the European Commission intervenes to purchase agricultural surpluses, thus supporting home markets and helping to achieve the average or *target price*.

intestacy Situation in which a person dies without making a valid will, leaving the estate without a designated heir. If a person dies intestate, the Crown divides the estate between the surviving relatives, making provision first for the spouse, and then for any children. If neither spouse nor children are living, other relatives are entitled to share in the estate. If no relatives can be traced, the estate goes to the Crown.

in transit Describing cash or goods that have been dispatched but not yet arrived. Items in transit have to be recorded in accounts if they have not arrived by the end of the accounting period.

intrinsic value Value of the materials from which an object is made, rather than its market or face value. For example, a coin may be said to be worth so much and is exchanged on the basis of that stated value, but the metal used in minting it (its intrinsic value) may be worth much less.

inventoriable costs Costs that are associated with products, stock or work in progress; i.e., ***product costs*** as opposed to ***distribution*** or ***selling costs***. The value of stock should be set at cost or net realizable value, whichever is the lower.

inventory List of the stock of raw materials, goods in production or finished goods owned and stored by a company, giving details of their cost, value and price. In the USA, the term inventory is synonymous with ***stock***.

inventory accounting Accounting system associated with the ordering, receipt and issuing of stock. It includes methods of ***stocktaking***.

inventory control Stock control. Most efficient businesses are managed, using inventories, in such a way that minimum levels of stock-in-trade sufficient to meet any likely demand are always maintained.

inventory equation Method of calculating the ending inventory, using the relationship: beginning inventory + net additions (purchases) – withdrawals (cost of goods sold) = ending inventory.

inventory turnover Also termed stock turnover, the number of times items of stock are used each accounting period (usually per year). For this period it equals the number of units used each year divided by the number of units in stock. Units in stock may be those at the beginning of the year, those at the end, or an average of the two.

inventory valuation Also termed stock valuation, the accumulated value of raw materials, work in progress and finished goods. The figures used should be cost or net realizable value, or costs accrued up to the present stage of production, whichever is the lower. *See also* ***stocktaking***.

investment Expenditure on real or financial assets rather than on funding of consumption. In this sense, expenditure consists of the purchase of any asset which is expected to increase in value. To an economist, however, investment covers spending that results in economic growth (such as money spent on the purchase of machinery or the building of plant that will produce goods and services for sale). In this sense, it extends to funds applied to the improvement of the infrastructure, and the term may also be applied to expenditure on human resources.

investment adviser Person who advises individuals or institutions on financial matters related to investment in its widest sense.

investment allowance Alternative term for ***capital allowance***.

investment centre Area of a company that is responsible for costs, revenues and any related investment. It may be as small as a section or as large as a subsidiary company.

investment costs Alternative term for ***capital costs***.

investment expenditure Alternative term for ***capital costs***.

investment grant Money made available by the government to companies for certain purposes.

investment income Company's income from outside investments (as opposed to revenue from normal business activities).

Investment Management Regulatory Organization (IMRO) Self-regulating UK organization set up under the Financial Services Act 1986 to regulate the activities of people or firms that give investment advice.

investment tax credit Incentive to investment in the USA. Part of the purchase price of an asset subject to depreciation can be offset against income tax in the year in which the purchase was made.

invisible asset *See* ***intangible asset***.

invoice Document that summarizes a business transaction and often doubles as a request for payment. An invoice lists and describes the goods (or services) ordered and details their price, and usually records the dates and times of dispatch and delivery.

invoice discounting Practice of offering a discount on unpaid invoices sold to a ***factoring*** company, which then tries to claim the money owed on its own account. The size of the discounting reflects the likely difficulty of securing payment.

IOSCO Abbreviation of ***International Organization for Securities Commissions***.

IRA Abbreviation of ***individual retirement account***.

IRR Abbreviation of ***internal rate of return***.

IRS Abbreviation of ***Internal Revenue Service***.

irrecoverable advanced corporation tax Part of advance corporation tax, already paid, that cannot be set against current gross corporation tax (GCT) nor carried back against gross corporation tax relating to the previous six years because it is larger than the maximum available set-off.

irrevocable input value added tax Input tax paid on goods purchased for producing ***exempt supplies***.

ISA Abbreviation of ***International Standards on Auditing***.

ITF Abbreviation of ***integrated test facility***.

J

JDS Abbreviation of ***Joint Disciplinary Scheme***.

JIT Abbreviation of ***just in time***.

job In business or industry, a particular project or piece of work, usually identified by means of a job number.

job card In costing a ***job***, a card on which is recorded the issues of parts or materials, hours of labour used, the cost of that labour and any associated overheads.

job cost Cost incurred in completing a ***job***, often broken down under such headings as direct labour costs, direct materials costs and overheads.

job costing Method of estimating the cost of completing a specific ***job***, also called specific order costing.

job cost sheet Alternative term for ***job card***.

job lot Collection of stocks or goods sold together, perhaps to somebody who wants only some of them.

job number Number assigned to an individual ***job*** under a job costing system.

job order Document detailing the costs assigned to a particular ***job*** or batch of jobs.

job-order costing Way of assigning costs to ***jobs*** that involve different amounts of attention and effort.

job-share Also known as time-share, employment that is held by two people, each working part-time.

job ticket Alternative term for ***job card***.

joint and several Concept by which joint debtors (for example, two or more partners in a partnership) are responsible for the debt, both jointly and as individuals. Joint and several liability gives the lender recourse to each of the partners in the debt in the event of default.

joint audit Audit performed by two or more auditors, for which the audit report is drawn up jointly.

Joint Disciplinary Scheme (JDS) Scheme established by the Institute of

Chartered Accountants in 1979 which regulates the conduct of members, especially in matters of public concern. It can impose sanctions on accounting firms that are found wanting.

joint product One of two or more products of similar value that are produced simultaneously by the same process.

joint production costs Costs of two or more products that are produced together by a single process and cannot be identified separately until a stage in production called the separation or split-off point. The costs are allocated to the individual products in accordance with their respective sales values at the separation point.

joint venture Situtation in which one (reporting) entity has a long-term contractual interest in another which is controlled jointly by the reporting entity and some other venture. The reporting entity details in its accounts with its share of assets, cash flows and liabilities of the joint venture.

journal Book in which daily transaction are recorded before being transferred to the books of account; the book of prime entry.

journal entry Record in a journal, with equal credits and debits, if necessary with an account of the transaction.

journal voucher Document detailing a transaction, before entry in a journal.

judgmental sampling In auditing, a type of sampling in which a sample is chosen from a population based on the auditor's own assessment and experience (rather than by statistical sampling).

just-in-time (JIT) Describing a method of supplying goods only to order immediately before they are required, so reducing stocks of raw materials and finished goods.

L

labour People used in the production of goods or services.

labour costs Also called wages costs, the expenses incurred in providing labour for the production process. In the UK, labour costs can include not only wages and salaries, but also National Insurance contributions and contributions to pension schemes. *See also* ***direct labour costs; indirect labour costs***.

labour efficiency variance *See* ***direct labour efficiency variance***.

labour hour rate Hourly rate of pay paid to workers categorized as direct labour or, in absorption costing, an absorption rate equal to the ratio of budgeted overheads to budgeted labour hours.

labour-intensive Describing a process, company or industry in which labour is the most significant and costly factor of production. Thus an industry in which the major cost is the payment of salaries, incentives and bonuses is labour-intensive.

labour variance *See* ***direct labour rate of pay variance***.

Laffer curve Diagram that illustrates a nonlinear relationship between tax rates and tax revenues for an economy, as popularized by Arthur Laffer.

land tax Tax on the ownership of land, normally paid in the form of ***rates***.

lapping US term for concealing a theft of or shortage of cash by delaying the recording of receipts of cash. For example, theft from one customer can be hidden by using the money received from the second customer; theft from the second is concealed by using money from the third; and so on. It is fraud, sometimes known in the UK as teeming and lading.

lapse To expire. For example, discounts not taken up by the stipulated time are said to lapse.

last in first out (LIFO) System of stock-keeping in which the latest items to be produced or bought are used or sold before old stock is cleared. In a period of deflation, this has the effect of maximizing profit, because new goods or material have cost less to produce or buy. *See also* ***first in first out (FIFO)***.

In the UK, the expression last in first out is also used to describe a method by which some companies make employees redundant, on the basis of length of service. Thus the last people to be employed are the first to be laid off.

laundering Method of disguising the origin of funds by moving them rapidly from one account or country to another. It thus becomes a complicated business to trace their origins, movements and eventual destination. Counterfeit money, stolen money or money received for illegal activities may be laundered.

laying-off Making an employee redundant, either temporarily or permanently, usually because there are insufficient orders for the whole workforce to be employed. *See also* ***last in last out***.

leading and lagging At the end of an accounting period, a method of improving a cash position and reducing borrowing by arranging for outstanding creditors to pay early (leading) while at the same time delaying the payment of debtors (lagging).

lead time Time that elapses between placing an order for goods or services and receiving them.

learning curve Recognition that, in most production processes, the time taken to produce one unit decreases as the quantity of production rises. It formula is $y = ax^{-b}$, where y is the average time per unit of production, x is the total number of units produced to date, a is the time taken to produce the first unit and b is the learning coefficient.

lease-back Arrangement by which a property is sold on condition that it is immediately leased back to the original owner. Capital tied up in the property is thereby released for other uses.

lease financing Type of off-balance sheet financing in which goods (for example, machinery) are leased rather than being purchased outright. Lease financing is therefore generally though of as a form of disguised borrowing.

least and latest rule US expression for minimizing the present value of tax payments by paying the least amount as late as possible (within the regulations).

ledger Book in which trade transactions, debits and credits are recorded. The term is most accurately applied to the principal volume in a series of account books, which collates the details made in books of original entry. Records may, of course, be held on computer records rather than hand-written in books.

ledger account Account in a ledger that records all transactions in a particular category, such as creditors, debtors, sales or stock.

legacy In computer science, an installation (hardware), application (software) or information (data) that already exists when a new one is introduced. A computerized accounting system, for example, has to be compatible with the legacy system (or, at great expense, the legacy system has to be scrapped altogther).

legal capital Stated value of the issued capital shares of a company. Under US state laws, it must remain permanently as protection for creditors (i.e., it cannot be diminished by paying dividends on shares).

legal charge See *charge*.

legal entity See *entity*.

legal tender Currency; notes or coins that may be offered as a medium of exchange. In the UK this means any number of banknotes, £2 or £1 coins; up to £10 in 50p or 20p coins; other 'silver' (cupro-nickel) coins to the value of £5; and 'copper' (bronze) coins to the value of 20p.

lender See *lending; loan*.

lending Temporarily granting of money, equipment, goods, people and so on, made on the understanding that the thing lent, or its equivalent, will be returned, sometimes with additional payment (interest).

letter of administration See *administrator*.

letter of engagement See *engagement letter*.

letter of representation Formal record of representations made by a company's management to its auditors (written by the auditor and signed by the management after the audit). It may refer to financial statements that the auditor has been unable to corroborate independently.

leverage Alternative, and mainly US, term for *gearing*.

leveraged company Company that is seriously in debt.

LIAB Abbreviation of Licentiate of the *International Association of Book-keepers*.

liabilities Company's or person's debts. Long-term (or deferred) liabilities are usually distinguished from current liabilities, as are secured debts from unsecured debts.

lien Right to possession of property until such time that an outstanding liability has been paid. A banker's lien gives a bank the right to retain or sell the property of a debtor in lieu of payment.

life-cycle costing Method of valuing an asset that takes into account its acquisition cost and its operating costs throughout its useful life.

LIFO Abbreviation of ***last in first out***.

LIFO reserve Current (or FIFO) cost of stock less it's historical cost.

limited company (Ltd) Also called a limited liability company, a company formed from a group of people whose liability is limited to the extent of the investment they have made (usually to purchase shares in the company), although occasionally limited liability is limited by guarantee to a certain amount as specified in the company's memorandum. *See also* ***public limited company***.

limited liability *See* ***limited company***.

limited partner Partner whose liability for the debts of the partnership is limited in law to the sum he or she invested in it. A limited partner does not generally share in the management of the firm. He or she may, however, offer advice and examine the books of account. ***See limited partnership***.

limited partnership Partnership in which one or more of the partners has only limited liability for the firm's debts. In each limited partnership there must be at least one general partner with unlimited liability. A limited partnership is therefore unpopular and a public limited company is preferred, because all shareholders in such a company have only limited liability. ***See general partnership***.

limited recourse financing Funds lent to a property development company, without the property being security for the lender (whose has recourse only to the developer's other assets in the event of default).

limiting factor Factor that restricts the production or sale of particular goods or services, such as the amount of labour available or production capacity. Limiting factors have to be eliminated if better levels of performance are to be achieved.

linear cost function Behaviour of costs that plotted against activity (such as production or sales) produce a straight-line graph.

linear depreciation Type of depreciation in which a constant amount is written off an asset each year. A graph of depreciation charges against time is a straight line.

line of credit Agreement with a financial institution (usually a bank) to accommodate short-term borrowings on demand.

liquid Describing something that is readily accessible, such as assets that can be immediately realized in cash form. Money is by definition fully liquid, and cash kept in a bank is the most obvious liquid asset. Treasury bills, money at call and Post Office savings are similarly liquid.

liquid assets Assets that consist of cash or can readily be converted into cash. They are also known by various other names, such as liquid capital, quick assets and realizable assets.

liquid assets ratio Ratio of the value of a company's assets that may be converted to cash without loss to its total assets.

liquidation Winding-up of a copmany, so-called because the company's assets are liquidated – converted into cash money – in order that outstanding creditors may be paid (in whole or, more usually, in part). In the USA the term is also used to denote payment of a debt.

liquidity Ease with which an asset can be converted into cash. Cash deposits in current bank accounts may be quickly withdrawn and are said to be highly liquid; money in most deposit accounts is slightly less liquid because notice must usually be given before withdrawal. Of a company, liquidity is the availability of cash (or near cash) to meet its debts and take advantage of investment opportunities.

liquidity index Method of measuring a company's liquidity in terms of the number of days it would take to convert current assets into cash.

liquidity risk In lending, the risk that an investment cannot, without substantial cost, be liquidated during its lifetime.

liquid ratio Alternative term for ***acid-test ratio***.

list price Published or quoted price for goods or services. *See also* ***discount***.

little GAAP Generally accepted accounting principles as they apply to small companies. *See* ***generally accepted accounting principles (GAAP)***.

loading Extra percentage added to interest on a loan to pay for administration charges or a higher risk than normal.

loan Sum of money borrowed by one person or organization from another on condition that it is repaid, generally for a specified time and often at an agreed rate of interest.

loan capital Another name for ***borrowed capital***.

loan creditor Person or organization from which a business has borrowed money.

loan rate Rate of interest charged for a loan, often expressed as a certain percentage above base rate.

local taxation Tax levied on people, businesses or their proerty in a particular area. The chief local taxes in the UK are business rates and council tax.

Lombard rate Interest rate used by the German central bank (the *Bundesbank*).

long-form report Detailed auditor's report on a person's or company's financial statements.

long-lived asset Asset that is expected to provide benefit for a number of years (such as investments and other intangible assets).

long-term contract accounting Accounting method of recognizing revenue as a percentage of completion of a long-term project (assuming the total revue on completion can be assessed).

long-term debtors Debtors who are unlikely to pay in the short term, which should be detailed on a company's balance sheet.

long-term liability Loans that do not have to be repaid in the current accounting period. The term is also sometimes used of debt that does not have to be repaid in the next three years.

loss Disadvantage, forfeiture of money or goods, or negative profit (the amount by which expenses of a transaction or project exceed income).

loss leader Product or service offered for sale at a substantial loss in order to attract customers. The hope is that people who buy the loss leader will also purchase other products from the same source.

loss on manufacture Also called production loss, a loss sustained when finished products leave production at a price that is less than the cost of producing them.

loss reliefs In certain circumstances, losses of companies, partnerships and sole traders can be set off against profits made or future profits. This is termed loss relief. If a company etc. ceases trading, terminal-loss relief may be available.

lowballing In auditing, a practice in which an auditor reduces his or her fees to get work (and beat the competition), usually compensated for by profitable non-audit consultancy work for the same client.

lower of cost and net realizable value rule Principle of valuing stock and work in progress at cost or net realizable value, whichever is the lower.

lower of cost and market Principle of valuing stock and work in progress at cost or market value (current replacement cost), whichever is the lower. *See also* ***basic rate; higher rate***.

lower rate Former rate of UK income tax, less than the basic rate, of 20%, payable on the first £4300 of taxable income. In April 1999 it was superseded by a starting rate tax of 10%, payable on the first £1500 of taxable income. *See also* ***basic rate; higher rate***.

lump sum Sum of money paid all at once, as opposed to being paid as a series of separate sums (instalments).

lump system System of payment under which workers receive a lump sum for each day's work or for the fulfilment of a daily quota. It is common in the building industry, but frowned upon because it can enable employees to avoid income tax.

luncheon voucher (LV) Voucher paid for by a company and issued to its employees which can be used in payment for food at participating outlets. Luncheon vouchers are not subject to income tax.

M

machine hour Method of measuring production in terms of the time a machine takes to produce a given amount of product.

machine hour rate In ***absorption costing***, the absorption rate equal to budgeted overheads divided by budgeted machine hours.

mail order System for buying and selling by post; the customer purchases goods or services directly from the manufacturer or distributor without the intervention of a middleman or retailer.

main product Most economically significant product of a process. *See also* ***by-product; joint product***.

mainstream corporation tax (MCT) ***Gross corporation tax*** less ***advance corporation tax*** (ACT) and any income tax deducted at source.

maintenance Practice of preserving the service potential of an asset (which is different from improvement or repair).

maintenance expense Cost of ***maintenance*** of assets, regarded as an overhead and allocated to the appropriate activity.

make-or-buy decision Decision whether to make a component or product within a company or to buy it in (from a subcontractor). It is usually based on cost as long as the company has the necessary manufacturing capacity. ***Opportunity costs*** should be considered if there is no capacity.

managed costs Alternative term for ***discretionary costs***.

management Control and supervision of a company, asset or operation; the group of people who control and administer a company, as distinct from the workforce. The effectiveness of a company's management is often of vital importance to its performance, and management is therefore sometimes regarded as a factor of production.

management accountant Accountant who is involved in the day-to-day running of a business, providing information upon which managers are able to base decisions. He or she assembles and processes financial information and data about quantities to enable cost control, pricing and, above all, decision making to happen. The distinction between cost accountants and management accountants is becoming increasingly blurred. *See also* ***cost accountant***.

management accounting Activity of a ***management accountant***.

management audit Audit carried out, usually by a management consultant, to check whether a company's management is functioning effectively.

management company Company whose business is management consultancy.

management discussion and analysis (MD&A) In the USA, the part of a company's annual report and accounts that explains financial changes that prevent direct comparison with previous years. It is similar in some respects to the ***operating and financial review*** in the UK.

management letter In auditing, letter from the auditor to a company's management suggesting possible benefits to the company, such as ways in which improvements might be made to financial systems.

managing director Senior executive director of a company, junior only to the chairman, and charged with implementing decisions made by the board of directors.

mandatory grant Grant that must be paid to all people and organizations that qualify for it (as opposed to a discretionary grant).

manufacturer's agent Agent who agrees to market a company's products, usually in a specific geographical area, in return for ***commission***.

manufacturing account Statement of account that forms part of the final accounts of a manufacturing company. Also known as a manufacturing statement, it includes manufacturing costs and overheads, and usually details profits and any losses.

manufacturing cost of finished goods Also called total production cost of finished goods, the sum of the ***prime cost*** and the ***manufacturing overhead***, adjusted to take into account any work in progress at the beginning and end of the accounting period.

manufacturing costs Also called manufacturing expenses or production costs, all expenses incurred by a manufacturer in the production of goods and services.

manufacturing expenses Alternative name for manufacturing costs, although in the USA the term is sometimes restricted to manufacturing overheads.

manufacturing loss Loss that occurs when the manufacturing costs of a product exceed the selling price (including cost of sales).

manufacturing overhead Also called production overhead, production costs that cannot be directly attributed to the product (usually everything but the direct costs). It includes cleansers and lubricants, depreciation of plant, maintenance costs, and business rent and rates.

manufacturing profit Profit that results when the manufacturing cost of a product is less than the selling price (including cost of sales).

manufacturing statement Alternative term for ***manufacturing account***.

manufacturing time Time it takes to produce a specific amount of product.

margin Part of the total cost of a product or service that represents the producer's profit, usually expressed as a percentage of revenue. Or, especially in the USA, a payment on account of a purchase which confers ownership with its attendant risks and privileges upon the buyer, but subjecting him or her to a lien on the purchase to the extent that credit is advanced to finance the full purchase price secured by the purchase.

marginal contribution Alternative term for ***contribution margin***.

marginal cost Cost incurred in raising the level of output by one unit beyond the original target (*see* ***marginal unit***). Marginal cost calculations are used to justify going beyond the target (or, indeed, not doing so).

marginal costing Alternative term for ***direct costing***.

marginal cost pricing Arriving at the selling price of a product by charging only marginal costs to it. It is seldom used except in times of intense competition.

marginal rate of tax Rate of corporation tax (levied on a company's profits) between the upper limit of £1,500,000 and the lower limit of £300,000 (figures are for 1999).

marginal relief Tax relief granted to a taxpayer whose income only marginally exceeds a specified level or tax bracket. He or she receives a proportion of the relief available to those in the lower bracket. The term is also applied to small companies relief, that is the relief in corporation tax available when a company's profits fall below the upper and lower limits (*see* ***marginal rate of tax***).

marginal revenue Revenue received by a company for selling one extra unit of product.

marginal unit Last unit produced, or the first to be supplied, defined as the smallest additional amount that is economically viable to produce or buy.

margin loan Also known as a top-up loan, a loan generally made on limited security. For example, a group of several lenders may advance money secured on property to 75% of its value. A margin loan would then be secured on the remaining 25%. This would carry a higher risk and therefore attract a slightly higher rate of interest.

margin of safety Amount by which actual or budgeted sales exceed breakeven sales, expressed in cash terms, percentage of capacity or units of production.

margin of safety ratio ***Margin of safety*** expressed as a percentage of a specified level of activity.

margin of solvency Amount by which a company's total assets are greater than its total liabilities (excluding share capital).

markdown Reduction in the selling price of goods, either below their marked up price (*see* ***markup***) or, in desperate times, below the retailer's purchasing price.

markdown cancellation Increase in selling price of goods by removal of earlier ***markdown***.

market capitalization Also termed market valuation, the value of all the securities of a company at current market prices.

marketing costs Cost to a company of marketing activities (cost of sales plus salespersons' salaries).

marketing cost variance Actual ***marketing costs*** less budgeted marketing costs for the same period.

marketing variance Difference between a ***flexible budget*** and a ***static budget***.

market price Also called market value, the price at which something is traded on the open market.

market rate Base interest rate charged for a loan. A spread is added to give the interest rate for a variable-rate loan.

market value Alternative term for ***market price***.

markup Increase above the acquisition cost made by a retailer to give a selling price that includes a profit. The retailer's markup is equal to gross profit.

M

markup cancellation Reduction in selling price of goods by removal of earlier additional ***markup***.

markup percentage Markup divided by selling price (= acquisition cost plus markup), expressed as a percentage.

master budget Alternative term for ***comprehensive budget***.

master budgeted sales Anticipated sales used in drawing up the comprehensive budget (master budget) for a period.

matching and cost recovery Method of either directly attributing expenses to associated revenues for a specific period or regarding them as costs that will not be recovered in a later period. Unexpired costs are carried as assets, not written off as expenses.

matching concept Also called the matching convention, the accounting principle of establishing a relationship between expenses and revenues for a specific period (so that profit and loss can be calculated).

material *See* ***direct materials; indirect materials***.

material adverse change In a loan agreement, a vague clause that requires the borrower to repay the loan if there is a material change in his or her financial circumstances.

material control Control of direct and indirect materials needed by a production process. Its aim is efficient stock control, with neither excess nor insufficient stocks being held.

materiality Relevance of accounting information, which should be included in financial statements if it is important for their understanding.

materials cost Cost of ***direct materials*** (part of prime cost) and ***indirect materials*** (part of manufacturing overheads).

materials oncost Additional costs that accrue through handling and storing ***direct materials***.

materials requisition Also termed stores requisition or, sometimes, a stores issue note, a document requesting that a particular item be issued from a company's stores (for a particular purpose). It is essential for efficient stock (inventory) control and accounting purposes.

materials returns note (MRN) Document that attests to the return of (unused) stock to a company's stores. It is essential for efficient stock (inventory) control and accounting purposes. It is also known as a stores returns note (SRN).

materials variances In standard costing, variances in price and quantity for direct materials. *See* ***direct materials total cost variance***.

material transfer note Document that records the transfer of material between different accounting codes.

matrix accounting Alternative to a T-account that employs a matrix to record accounting events and transactions.

maximum stock level Highest planned quantity of stock (inventory), over which the stock is considered to be in excess.

MCT Abbreviation of ***mainstream corporation tax***.

MD&A Abbreviation of ***management discussion and analysis***.

medium-sized company Company that, because of its size, is allowed certain exemptions in filing accounts. Two of the following criteria must apply: total assets (balanace-sheet total) should be less than £5,600,000; turnover should be less than £11,200,000; there should be fewer than 250 employees on average.

memorandum entry Ledger entry that is not part of a double-entry book-keeping system.

mercantile agent Person or company that takes part in ***factoring***.

merchandise Finished goods that are purchased by a wholesaler or retailer for resale.

merchandise turnover Stock (inventory) turnover for merchandise.

merchandising business Business that purchases finished goods for resale (as opposed to a manufacturing business).

merger accounting When two or more businesses combine, a method of accounting that treats them equally (as if they had always been merged).

mezzanine finance Money lent to a small and growing, but financially viable, company. It is so called because the risk of making the loan falls between that of advancing ***venture capital*** and the safer course of putting the finance into the established debt market.

MIAS Abbreviation of Member of the ***Institute of Accounting Staff***.

middleman Intermediary, usually a wholesaler, retailer or broker, who acts as an agent between a buyer and a seller. Middlemen tend to push up prices by adding their own profit margin to the difference between the buying and selling prices, and it may therefore be in the interests of the buyer and seller to 'cut out the middleman' (as, for example, in mail order).

minimum wage Lowest amount a company may pay a worker, often fixed by legislation or trade union agreements.

minority interest Interest held by shareholders in a subsidiary company (excluding the holding company's interest).

minutes book Details of all decisions made by a company's board of directors or at shareholders' meetings.

MIRAS Abbreviation of ***mortgage interest relief at source***.

misdeclaration penalty In accounting for UK value added tax (VAT), a penalty of 15% of the VAT lost in understating VAT liability or overstating VAT refund due. It applies if the inaccuracy is 30% of the total VAT due or £1 million, whichever is the lesser.

misrepresentation Any false statement that encourages a person or company to enter into a contract. It may be either fraudulent, i.e., a deliberate intention to deceive, or innocent, i.e., the result of a genuine mistake. Under UK law the injured party may have the contract dissolved and claim substantial damages. *See also* ***mistake***.

mistake Legally, any error, short of ***misrepresentation***, that induces a person or company to enter into a contract. Mistakes may be mutual, i.e., common to both parties, or unilateral. Mutual mistakes include the innocent purchase or exchange of goods that are not in fact for sale; unilateral mistakes include more deliberate deceptions. Both mutual and unilateral mistakes may invalidate a contract, but they do not necessarily do so. *See also* ***accounting errors***.

mixed cost Cost that has both fixed and variable components. *See* ***fixed cost; variable cost***.

mix variance In standard costing, a direct materials variance that occurs when a product is produced using several different raw materials. It arises because the actual mix of materials used is different from the standard mix budgeted for.

modified accounts Alternative term for ***abbreviated accounts***.

modified historical cost convention Variation of ***historical cost accounting*** that allows certain assets to be revalued (as opposed to being included at their acquisition cost).

modified cash basis Variation of ***cash basis*** accounting in which long-term assets may be accounted for on an ***accrual basis***.

monetary assets Also known as monetary items, assets with a fixed exchange value for money and are unaffected by changes in price levels (such as accounts receivable, cash and debtors).

monetary items Alternative term for ***monetary assets***.

monetary measurement convention Accounting convention that a financial statement records a transaction only if it can be expressed in monetary terms. As a result, highly trained and reliable staff or extremely valuable ***goodwill*** are not accounted for.

money Medium of exchange; any generally accepted token that may be exchanged for goods or services, a unit of account and ideally a store of value (but *see* ***inflation***). *See also* ***legal tender***.

money of account Denomination of money that, although no longer produced (such as the guinea in the UK), is still used in keeping some accounts.

moratorium Grant of an extended peiod in which to repay a loan, or a period during which the repayment schedule is suspended.

MRN Abbreviation of ***materials returns note***.

mortgage Transfer of the deeds to a property as security for the repayment of a debt. For example, a building society that provides a loan for the purchase of a house takes legal possession of the property until the loan and interest have been repaid. The lender is the mortgagee; the borrower is the mortgagor. A mortgage is also called a legal charge.

mortgage bond Bond that, in the USA, represents a debt secured by a real asset.

mortgagee *See* ***mortgage***.

mortgage interest relief at source (MIRAS) Former income tax relief allowed to a UK taxpayer on the first £30,000 of a mortgage on his or her main residence. Set at 10% for the year 1999-2000, it was abolished in April 2000.

mortgagor *See* ***mortgage***.

multicolumn reporting Drawing up of accounts in several ways under separate columns that stand for a different basis (such as historical cost convention, replacement cost, and so on).

multinational corporation Corporation that has offices and operations in more than one country.

M

multiple Chain store; a group of shops in numerous locations selling the same stock under one management group. Or it is the factor by which the cost of producing one unit of goods is multiplied to arrive at a satisfactory selling price.

multiple breakeven points More than one activity level at which a company breaks even (because the non-linear total cost and total revenue curves cross more than once on the breakeven chart).

mutual Describing a company owned by its depositors or members but which does not issue stocks or shares. In the UK, some building societies and insurance companies have this status.

N

NAA Abbreviation of ***National Association of Accountants***.

NAO Abbreviation of ***National Audit Office***.

National Association of Accountants (NAA) US organization concerned mainly with management accounting. The largest organization of its type, most of its members are not certified public accountants.

National Audit Office (NAO) Organization established in the UK in 1983 that audits the accounts of government departments and checks on their financial effectiveness.

National Insurance Tax levied in the UK, nominally to pay for social security benefits and retirement pensions. It is paid by employers, employees and self-employed persons.

natural business year Company accounting period of 12 months selected in such a way that the end of the period coincides with low activity or low stocks.

natural classification Method of classifying expenses in terms of the nature of items acquired, such as depreciation, insurance, materials, salaries and taxes. *See also* ***functional classification***.

natural wastage Method of reducing the workforce of a company without resorting to enforced redundancies. As far as possible, the employer does not replace staff who die, retire or resign.

NAV Abbreviation of ***net asset value***.

NBV Abbreviation of net book value; *see* ***depreciated cost***.

negative cash flow Cash flow in which outgoings are greater than income.

negative confirmation *See* ***confirmation***.

negative equity Asset that is currently worth less than the money borrowed to pay for it. *See* ***equity***.

negative income tax (NIT) System of taxation in which those earning less than a specified income receive tax credits to bring their income in line with a guaranteed minimum income.

negligible value Description of an asset of little or no value.

negotiated market price Price agreed between a buyer and a seller where there is no established market to fix a price.

net That which remains after all deductions and charges have been made. *See also* **gross**.

net annual value *See* ***annual value***.

net assets Difference between a company's assets and its liabilities (sometimes termed owners' equity).

net asset value (NAV) Value of a company's shares determined by dividing its net assets by the number of issued shares. It is seldom the same as the market value.

net book value (NBV) Alternative term for ***depreciated cost***.

net cash flow In any accounting period, the difference between cash entering a company and cash leaving it. *See* ***cash flow***.

net current assets Difference between current assets and current liabilities, equal to a company's working capital.

net income For a given accounting period, the amount by which all revenues and gains exceed all expenses and losses. It is also called net gain.

net loss For a given accounting period, the amount by which all expenses and losses exceed all revenues and gains; sometimes called negative net income.

net margin Difference between the selling price of an item and the total cost of making and selling it.

net markup For retail stock (inventory), all ***markups*** minus markup cancellations (usually ignoring ***markdowns***).

net monetary position Company's total monetary assets less total monetary liabilities.

net present value (NPV) In a discounted cash flow, the present value of cash outflows from a company less the present value of cash inflows. The worth of a future project can be assessed by discounting all future cash flows to the present to see if a desired rate of return would be achieved. A negative NPV would indicate that the project is not viable.

net price method Method of recording sales (or purchases) at the invoice price minus any available discounts (because discounts are nearly always taken).

net profit Company's income that remains after deducting all expenses.

net profit ratio Ratio of net profit to sales (turnover), expressed as a percentage.

net realizable value (NRV) Amount that could be obtained for an asset (less direct selling costs). Or sales value of a company's stock (less cost of sales). Both may be less that actual cost.

net residual value Alternative term for ***disposal value***.

netting off Deducting a provision from an accounting item (such as provisions for bad and doubtful debts).

net worth Value of a company after liabilities have been deducted from the true market value of its assets.

next in first out (NIFO) Method of valuing raw materials or finished goods in stock in terms of the next unit price that will have to be paid (in practice the replacement cost).

NIFO Abbreviation of ***next in first out***.

nil-rate band Amount of a person's estate (the first £234,000 in 2000/01) that is not subject to ***inheritance tax***.

NIT Abbreviation of ***negative income tax***.

nominal accounts One of the three parts into which a book-keeping ledger is divided. The nominal accounts are the records of income and expenditure. *See also* ***impersonal accounts; personal accounts; real accounts; temporary accounts***.

nominal ledger Alternative term for ***general ledger***.

nominal price Minimal price assigned to an item so that a transaction may be accounted for.

nominal value Alternative term for ***face value***.

non-adjusting event Any event that occurs after a company's balance sheet has been dated but before its financial statements have been approved by its directors. If significant it should be included in the notes to the accounts.

non-controllable costs Expenditure that a manager cannot control or influence (although a more senior manager may be able to do so).

N

noncurrent Describing something that is due in more than one year's time.

non-equity share Share in a company that restricts its owner's participation in any surplus on liquidation to a specified amount (not related to assets or profits), or that limits its owner's receipts of payments to a specified amount (not related to assets or profits, or to dividends paid on any equity shares), or that can be redeemed according to its stated terms or because its owner wants to redeem it.

nonexpendable fund In the USA, a government fund whose principal (and sometimes revenue) cannot be spent.

nonmonetary item Any item that is not monetary (*see* ***monetary item***).

nonoperating Describing expenses and revenues resulting from activities that are only incidental to a company's main line of business.

non-performing asset Asset (part of a company's capital) that is currently yielding no return, and on which none is expected. Fixed assets are generally classified as non-performing.

non-production overhead costs Company's indirect costs that are not regarded as part of manufacturing overheads, such as overheads associated with administration, distribution and selling.

non-profit making organization (NPO) Company or organization that has a legal obligation not to make a profit. The term is most usually applied to registered charities.

non-purchased goodwill Goodwill generated from within an organization, not acquired with it.

non-recourse finance Loan in which the lender is entitled to repayment only from the profits of the venture the loan is funding (and not from any other assets the borrower may have).

non-statistical sampling Alternative term for ***judgmental sampling***.

non-statutory accounts Formerly called abridged accounts, company accounts that deal with a financial period that does not form part of the statutory accounts.

non-taxable income Income which for one reason or another is not subject to normal income tax. In the UK it includes proceeds from gambling, money received by charities, some social security benefits and redundancy pay.

normal activity Rate of company activity needed to meet sales demand averaged over a period that is long enough to include any cyclical and seasonal variations.

normal capacity Capacity of company production as budgeted for a stated period, expressed in direct labour hours, standard hours or machine hours.

normal costing Method of estimating production costs that employs actual direct materials used, actual direct labour employed, and budgeted overhead rates.

normal loss Loss that results from a manufacturing process because of expected seepage, shrinkage, spoilage or other forms of waste. Such losses are included in normal manufacturing costs.

normal shrinkage *See **normal loss**.*

normal spoilage *See **normal loss**.*

normal standard cost *See **normal costing**.*

normal volume Production level over a period (usually a year) that will satisfy sales demand; the budgeted volume for that period, used to calculate the overhead absorption rate.

normal waste *See **normal loss**.*

normative theories of accounting Accounting theories that define procedures and policies, usually derived by deductive reasoning.

note of hand Alternative term for a ***promissory note***.

note of historical cost profits and loss Memorandum in a company's annual report and accounts that restates the profit and loss account in shortened form but ignoring any revaluations (if these have been significant).

notes to the accounts Additional information in support of a company's financial statements (such as data on fixed assets, investments and reserves).

notes payable Promissory notes that prove the existence of a debt and state the terms under which it is to be repaid.

not for profit organization In the USA, an organization (such as a charity) that provides goods or services on which no profit is made. It is equivalent to a ***non-profit making organization*** in the UK.

NPO Abbreviation of ***non-profit making organization***.

NPV Abbreviation of ***net present value***.

NRV Abbreviation of ***net realizable value***.

number fudging Alternative term for ***creative accounting***.

number of days' stock held Ratio that measures the average number of days' stock being held by a company, equal to 365 times the number of units in stock divided by the number of units of stock used in a year. The number in stock may be those at the beginning or end of the year, or an average of the two figures. In the USA it is usually termed number of days' sales in inventory.

O

objective function Company aim that can be quantified, such as to minimize costs or to maximize profit, according to the availability of the factors of production. It is also known as the choice criterion in the USA.

objectives of financial statements of financial statements in a company's annual report and accounts, that is, principally to provide data to enable decisions to be made.

objectivity Accounting principle that anyone who prepares accounts should make no subjective assessments, an advantage sometimes claimed for historical cost accounting.

object of costing *See* ***cost objective***.

OBSF Abbreviation of ***off balance sheet finance***.

obsolescence Loss of the value of something when it becomes out of date. In accounting, obsolescence refers to an asset that has to be written off, not through deterioration but when its continued use would be uneconomic. For example, a piece of machinery may be superseded by a new, faster version; it is therefore uneconomic for the company to continue to use it, and the asset becomes obsolete. *See also* ***wear and tear; write off***.

off balance sheet finance (OBSF) Type of company finance such that some or all of it (and associated assets) do not appear on the company's balance sheet. Although legally allowable, the practice can give a very distorted view of a company's financial status.

offset account Account that reduces the total of another account to produce a net balance.

OMV Abbreviation of ***open-market value***.

on account Describing a sale (or purchase) for which no payment is expected until some time after delivery; on credit.

on consignment Describing goods sent by their owner (consignor) to an agent (consignee) to be sold by the agent. The consignor is entitled to payment of a pre-agreed amount or return of the goods if they are not sold.

oncost Additional expense, such as that from employing staff (wages oncost) or storing goods (storage oncost). The term has also been used a synonym of ***overheads***.

open account Trade between an exporter and importer without any built-in guarantee of payment. The exporter submits an invoice and expects to be paid in due course, as is the case with a normal domestic transaction.

open indent Order for goods that does not specify a particular supplier. The agent receiving the indent may purchase suitable goods from any manufacturer at his or her own discretion.

opening balance At the beginning of an accounting period, the balance (debit or credit) that is brought forward.

opening entries First journal entries made when a business begins trading, including assets, capital and liabilities.

opening stock At the beginning of an accounting period, any raw materials, work in progress or finished goods held in stock by a company. It is equivalent to the closing stock of the previous period.

open market Market in which goods are available to be bought and sold by anyone who cares to. Prices on an open market are determined by the laws of supply and demand.

open-market value (OMV) Asset's value regarded as the amount someone would be willing to pay for it.

operating Describing expenses and revenue associated with a company's main line of business.

operating accounts In cost accounting, accounts that deal with day-to-day expenses, revenues and production costs.

operating and financial review Statement forming part of a company's annual accounts and report in which the directors explain the financial figures and discuss – positively or negatively – business financing and opportunities/risks facing the company.

operating budget Alternative term for ***cash budget***.

operating costs Costs incurred in the day-to-day running of a business.

operating costing Type of costing that deals with providing services within a company, or with the operation of continuous processes, such as power generation.

operating cycle Time taken, on average, between buying goods or services

O

and being paid for their subsequent re-sale. It is also called the working-capital cycle.

operating expenses Alternative term for ***operating costs***.

operating margin Operating profit expressed as a proportion of price or operating costs. It is also called ***current gross margin***.

operating performance ratio Any of several ratios used to measure a company's financial performance in a given period, usually in terms of the returns on sales in that period (such as its gross margin).

operating profit or loss Profit or loss made by a company through its main activity, calculated by taking operating costs away from trading profit (or adding operating expenses to its trading loss). It excludes interest on loans, returns on other investments, or any other extraordinary items.

operating risk Risk that a process, once begun, will not continue to be as productive as predicted.

operation Another term for a business (such as a company, partnership or firm) or an activity it undertakes.

operation costing Method of costing in which material costs and conversion costs are re-calculated for each batch of production.

operational audit Assessment of a company's effectiveness through a complete review of all of its activities.

operational variances In standard costing, the difference between targets set and what is actually achieved under current operating conditions.

opinion Alternative term for an ***auditor's report***.

opinion shopping Colloquial term for 'shopping around' to find an auditor who will give a favourable opinion on a company's financial policy.

opportunity cost Revenue foregone by using an asset for one purpose rather than another. For example, a company owning a building which it uses as storage space could rent it to someone else. That rent is the opportunity cost of the building.

OR Abbreviation of official receiver. *See* ***receivership***.

order-filling cost Cost incurred in collecting, storing, packing, transporting, invoicing and other aspects of selling goods.

order-getting cost Cost incurred in attaining the required volume and mix of goods for selling.

ordinary activities Activities, and any related activities, carried out by a company in pursuance of its normal business.

ordinary incremental budget Budget prepared by changing figures in the previous period's budget in line with experience during that period and bearing in mind what the future is expected to hold.

organization costs Costs incurred in setting up an accounting entity, a type of intangible asset although it is often treated as an expense in the initial period.

original cost Cost of something when it is purchased; acquisition cost.

original entry Accounting entry in a book of prime entry (journal).

original entry error Error in a book of prime entry (journal). A trial balance fails to reveal such errors.

originating timing difference Difference between profits (or losses) arrived at for taxation purposes, when receipts and payments are recorded on the dates they are made, and profits (or losses) calculated on an accruals basis for a company's financial statements. The tax calculations may therefore relate to a different period from that of the financial statement.

outgoings Alternative term for ***expenditure***.

outlay Alternative term for ***expenditure***.

outlay cost Expenditure incurred in setting up an activity or project; origination cost.

out-of-pocket Describing expenditure normally met using cash, or an ***incremental cost*** that follows a particular decision.

out-of-stock cost Loss of future profit resulting from a company being unable to fulfil orders because of lack of stock.

output Amount produced by a company, single person or a machine.

output tax Value added tax (VAT) charged (on taxable goods or services) by a trader registered for VAT. Since April 1991 the standard rate in the UK has been 17.5%, except for zero-rated goods (such as books) and exempt supplies (such as financial and postal services).

outstanding Describing something that is unpaid (such as cheque that has been issued but not credited to an account) or that is uncollected (such as a debt).

overabsorbed overhead In absorption costing, a situation in which the absorbed overhead is larger than the actual overhead costs for a given period. This favourable variance increases budgeted profits.

over-and-short US term for an expense account that records slight differences between a book balance of cash and actual money held in petty cash.

overapplied overhead US term for ***overabsorbed overhead***.

overcapitalization Situation in which a company has more capital than it can employ to its profit. *See also* ***gearing.***

overhead Costs incurred in the everyday running of a business and not variable according to its output. Also known as indirect costs, fixed costs or supplementary costs, or 'burden' in the USA, overhead costs include heating, lighting and energy costs, administration, insurance, rent and rates. Cost of sales and research and development costs are also usually included.

overhead absorption *See* ***absorption***.

overhead absorption rate *See* ***absorption rate***.

overhead analysis sheet Also called an overhead distribution summary, a document used to allocate manufacturing overhead to the appropriate costs centres.

overhead cost *See* ***overhead***.

overhead cost absorbed For a given period, the actual production achieved times the budgeted overhead absorption rate.

overhead distribution summary Alternative term for ***overhead analysis sheet***.

overhead efficiency variance Also termed overhead productivity variance or simply productivity variance, in standard costing a variance that arises because available production time is used more efficiently. It is equal to the standard production hours budgeted less the actual hours taken, multiplied by the variable overhead absorption rate per hour.

overhead expenditure variance *See* ***expenditure variance***.

overhead expenses Term sometimes used for indirect expenses, sometimes for fixed costs, and sometimes for both. Its precise meaning varies from company to company. *See* ***overhead***.

overhead productivity variance Alternative term for ***overhead efficiency variance***.

overhead total variance In standard costing, the difference between recovered overhead and incurred overhead for a given period.

overhead volume variance *See **fixed overhead volume variance***.

overtrading Describing a potentially dangerous situation in which a company tries to take on more business than its working capital will allow.

P

paid-in capital In the USA, owners' equity in a company, i.e., the total amount invested during and since its incorporation.

paid-in surplus In the USA, excess received by a company over and above the par (standard) value of its issued shares.

paid-up share capital Capital obtained by a company for a share issue in which the shares are fully paid.

P & L Abbreviation of ***profit and loss account***.

paper company Company established, usually with little capital, merely for financial purposes. *See also* ***shell company***.

paper profit Gain that has not yet been realized by the completion of a transaction or because the value of an asset has fallen.

parent company Company that own or part-owns, but more importantly controls, one or more subsidiary companies. *See also* ***holding company***.

partial exemption In value added tax (VAT), a restriction on the amount of input tax that can be set against output tax because a trader deals in a mixture of exempt goods or services and taxable goods or services.

partial obsolescence State of an out-of-date asset which cannot, however, have an accounting loss attributed to it (although it may be depreciated). *See* ***obsolescence***.

participative budgeting Involvement of management in drawing up a budget, against which its performance may later be measured.

particular lien Right to take possession of specified assets in the event of default. It relates only to the debt arising from the asset over which the lien is held.

partner Person engaged in a business enterprise jointly with, and generally with the same staus and responsibilities as, another or others. *See* ***partnership***.

partner's drawing Payment to a partner, which is charged against his or her share of revenue.

partnership Business association, in the UK normally formed between two to twenty partners. The partners are jointly liable for the debts of the partnership, so that if one partner dies or decamps, the remainder are responsible for any debts. *See also* ***general partnership***; ***limited partnership***.

par value Alternative term for ***face value***.

payable In US usage, describing something (such as an invoice) that is unpaid but not necessarily due to be paid or overdue. In UK usage, the term usually means due to be paid.

payables Informal term for a company's short-term debts (debtors).

pay and file Former method of dealing with corporation tax, introduced in the UK at the end of September 1993. A company had to file detailed tax returns within a year of the end of an accounting period, although tax was due after nine months. Self-assessment replaced pay and file after 1 July 1999.

pay-as-you-earn (PAYE) System of income tax collection in the UK in which tax is deducted from current earnings at source. The employer is responsible for collecting the tax, and the employee receives only net wages. A similar system is called pay-as-you-go in the USA.

payback period Time that elapses before a new project's cash inflows equal its cash outflows. In the USA it is also called payoff or payout.

payback period method Method in which the anticipated ***payback period*** of a project is compared to the required payback period, in order to decide whether or not to go ahead with the project. For a project with constant annual cash inflows, the payback period (in years) equals the initial capital investment divided by the annual cash inflow.

PAYE Abbreviation of ***pay-as-you-earn***.

payment in advance Payment for goods or services made before they are received. Under the accruals concept, it is accounted for as a deferred debit.

payment in kind Payment, generally of wages, made in goods or services rather than in money. Payment of total wages in kind was made illegal in the UK in the 19th century, but part-payment in kind still occurs (for example, luncheon vouchers and the use of a company car are payments in kind).

payment on account Part payment of an outstanding debt, usually coupled with an agreement to repay the balance by a specific date. For long-term contract work, payment on account (also called progress payment) denotes a stage payment for work completed by a certain specified time.

payoffs US term for outcomes, i.e., the consequences of various possible actions or events. *See also* ***payback period***.

payout *See* ***payback period***.

payroll List of people employed (usually full-time) by a company and of the amount that each is due to be paid.

payroll tax Tax on a business undertaking levied in relation to the number of people employed, or as a percentage of the total wages bill. It is sometimes used to control the relative elasticities of the supply and demand for labour. Its imposition deters companies from employing more workers than they currently require.

PCTCT Abbreviation of profits chargeable to ***corporation tax***.

peculation ***Embezzlement***, particularly the appropriation of public money or goods by an official.

P/E ratio Abbreviation of ***price-earnings ratio***.

per books US term for the ***book value*** of an asset or other item.

per capita Latin for 'by the head'. It usually indicates that a sum will be divided equally among a group. Thus per capita income is calculated by dividing the total income received by a group by the number of people in the group.

percentage depletion Alternative term for ***depletion allowance***.

percentage of completion Method of estimating expenses or revenues from a job (particularly a long-term contract) over a particular period in proportion to the costs thus far incurred divided by the total estimated cost, or in proportion to the amount of work that has been completed.

percentage on direct labour cost In absorption costing, method of absorbing the production overhead into the product. It is equal to 100 times the budgeted production overhead divided by the budgeted direct labour cost.

percentage on direct material cost In absorption costing, method of absorbing the manufacturing overhead into the product. It is equal to 100 times the budgeted manufacturing overhead divided by the budgeted direct material cost.

percentage on prime cost In absorption costing, method of absorbing the manufacturing overhead into the product. It is equal to 100 times the budgeted manufacturing overhead divided by the budgeted prime cost.

per contra Latin for 'by the opposite side'. In accounting, it indicates an entry on the opposite side of an account or balance sheet. It is therefore a self-balancing item.

per diem Latin for 'by the day'. It usually applies to an allowance, rental or other charge made on a daily basis.

performance ratio See ***financial ratio***.

performance report Document that compares a budget with actual results.

performance standard In standard costing, a specified level of performance that is to be attained in a given period.

period In the context of accounting, usually an accounting period.

period concept Concept that a company's financial statements should be drawn up at regular periods (often annually).

period costs Also termed period expenses, costs charged to operations during an accounting period because they are incurred with the passage of time (such as rent and rates).

period expenses Alternative term for ***period costs***.

periodic inventory Alternative (mainly US) term for ***periodic stocktaking***.

periodic stocktaking Evaluating or counting stock at the end of an accounting period.

period of account Time period for which a company's accounts are drawn up (usually a year).

perishable goods Goods that are likely to deteriorate over a relatively short period of time. The term is most frequently applied to foodstuffs.

perks Abbreviation of perquisites, i.e., casual benefits. In general terms perks are ***payments in kind***, but are more specifically applicable to informal rather than formal agreed benefits.

permanent account Account that appears on a company's balance sheet (as opposed to a temporary account).

permanent difference Difference between profits (or losses) calculated for purposes of taxation and profits (or losses) as they appear on a company's financial statements. For example, entertainment expenses cannot be deducted from profit for tax purposes.

permanent diminution in value Irreversible decrease in the value of an asset.

perpetual audit Alternative term for ***continuous inventory***.

perpetual debt On-going debt for which the issuer does not repay the principal, generally just constant-rate interest (or interest tied to a benchmark rate).

perpetual inventory Alternative term for ***continuous inventory***.

perpetual succession Continuation of a company after the departure or death of its members. A company is an individual legal entity which exists irrespective of its personnel, and which ceases to exist in law only after its liquidation.

persistent misdeclaration penalty Penalty for significant inaccuracy of a UK value added tax (VAT) return of £500,000 or 10% of the correct amount, whichever is the lower. The penalty is 15% of the 'lost' VAT.

personal account In book-keeping, an account that lists creditors and debtors.

personal allowance Amount that a person may earn before he or she is liable to pay income tax.

Personal Investment Authority (PIA) A UK self-regulatory organization (SRO) established in 1993 that oversees businesses that deal with private investors. It is a self-regulating organization (SRO) and took over responsibilities from the Financial Intermediaries, Managers and Brokers Regulatory Organization (FIMBRA) and the Life Assurance and Unit Trust Regulatory Organization (LAUTRO). In 1997 it was itself incorporated into the Financial Services Authority (FSA).

personal ledger Ledger that contains personal accounts (such as creditors and debtors).

PET Abbreviation of ***potentially exempt transfer***.

petties Abbreviation of ***petty cash***, used most commonly on an invoice to denote charges for various small items not separately enumerated.

petty cash Money in notes and coins kept for payment of small bills and day-to-day expenses. *See also* ***float***.

petty cash book Book in which ***petty cash*** transactions are recorded.

physical capital maintenance *See* ***capital maintenance concept***.

physical inventory Also known as a physical stock check, the counting of remaining items in stock as part of a stocktaking exercise.

physical stock check Alternative term for ***physical inventory***.

physical verification Auditor's verification of stock, assets, and so on by his or her physically checking them (as opposed to merely checking written accounts). The auditor may use a statistical sampling procedure.

PI Abbreviation of ***profitability index***.

PIA Abbreviation of ***Personal Investment Authority***.

piece rate Payment to a worker based on his or her level of output (how many 'pieces' he or she makes). *See* ***piecework***.

piecework Work that is paid per unit of output (instead of per hour of time worked). By linking earnings to output, the worker is given an incentive to increase productivity. *See also* ***piece rate***.

planning, programming, budgeting system (PPBS) Budgeting system used by charities, local government, and other non-profit making organizations. Activities with common objectives are grouped together, and a long-term overall plan (split into individual programmes) is drawn up.

planning variance In standard costing, a variance to adjust the basic standard if circumstances have changed materially since it was first set. It is also known as revision variance.

plant Fixtures or machinery used in an industrial process (i.e., tangible fixed assets), or a general term for a factory or industrial complex.

plant and equipment *See* ***plant***.

plant and machinery *See* ***plant***.

plant assets Alternative term for ***plant***.

plant register Register that lists the ***plant*** owned by a company. A record is kept of purchase price, running costs, current worth and annual depreciation. It may also be called an assets register or fixed-assets register.

plc Abbreviation of ***public limited company*** (sometimes rendered as Plc or PLC).

pledging Mainly US term for assigning assets as collateral or security for a loan. The term is retained in the UK with regard to pawnbroking. Legal ownership of the asset remains with the pledger.

pledging of receivables Mainly US term for using expected amounts receivable as collateral for a loan.

ploughed-back profit Company revenues that are retained for continued investment in the business, more usually known as ***retained earnings***.

plugging US term for determining an unknown amount by applying the accounting equation: opening balance + additions – deductions = closing balance (if any three of these are known the fourth can be deduced).

pooling of interest method US method of accounting for a business combination in which the assets and equities of the combined firms are merely added together. No matter what the date of acquisition, net income is recognized for the full financial year.

positive accounting theory Theory that attempts to explain why accounting policies and procedures are what they currently are (unlike ***normative theories of accounting***).

positive confirmation *See* ***confirmation***.

post To enter records in an account or ledger (often transferred from a journal).

post-balance-sheet events Alternative term for ***adjusting events***.

post-cessation receipts Sums received for an activity after the activity has ceased. They may be accounted for tax purposes in the year the activity ceased or in the year of receipt.

post-closing trial balance Trial balance made after temporary accounts have been closed.

post-dated *See* ***forward dating***.

post-statement events Significant events that occur after the end of an accounting period but before financial statements are published. They have to be disclosed to the auditor.

potentially exempt transfer (PET) Lifetime gift that is not liable to ***inheritance tax*** as long as the donor lives for at least seven years after the date of the gift. If the donor dies within seven years, tax depends on the size of the gift and when it was made.

practical capacity Maximum level at which a company department or production process can work most efficiently (with due allowance for unavoidable interruptions).

Practice Notes Notes regarding good auditing practice issued by the ***Auditing Practices Board (APB)***.

pre-acquisition profits Profits made by a company before it was taken over by another one.

preclosing trial balance Trial balance made at the end of an accounting period but before entries are finally closed.

predetermined overhead rate In absorption costing, an overhead rate determined at the beginning of a new process or operation, using budgeted figures for costs and output.

preliminary announcement Also called preliminary statement, an announcement of a company's full year results a month or two before publication of its annual report.

preliminary expenses Expenses incurred in setting up a new company (such as the cost of printing share certificates and issuing them).

preliminary statement Alternative term for ***preliminary announcement***.

prepaid expenses Expenditure that results in a prepayment or deferred charge. For example, insurance premiums or rents already paid continue to provide benefit in the future (and as such are assets).

prepaid income Alternative term for an ***advance*** from a customer or client (it does not become revenue until the goods or services are delivered).

prepayment *See* ***payment in advance***.

present value Alternative term for ***discounted value***.

present-value factor Alternative term for ***discount factor***.

pre-tax profit Profit calculated before allowance has been made for tax.

price Cost of purchasing a unit of goods or services. Very broadly, prices are generally set by the producer and retailer, taking into account all fixed costs and variable costs and allowing for a profit margin. *See also* ***fair market price***.

price-earnings ratio (P/E ratio) Current market price of a company's ordinary shares divided by the earnings per share.

pricing Method used to set a selling ***price***, often by equating supply with demand.

price index Series of numbers that represent average prices over a period of time, relative to a base (usually 100 or 1000) assigned to the first period. *See* ***Retail Price Index (RPI)***.

P

price level Price from a ***price index*** for a given date or period.

price-level accounting Theoretical method of accounting that would take into account changes in price levels over time (unlike historical cost accounting).

price variance In standard costing, the difference between actual and standard cost per unit multiplied by the quantity purchased. It is also termed value variance. *See also* ***direct materials price variance***.

primary auditor When group accounts are being drawn up, the auditor of the holding company. *See also* ***secondary auditor***.

primary capital Capital that is used to start up a business. *See also* ***venture capital***.

primary distribution Distribution of raw materials to manufacturers.

primary production Production of raw materials and foodstuffs. *See also* ***secondary production***.

prime cost Combined cost of direct expenses, direct labour and direct materials, as assigned to a product.

prime documents Documents that give rise to entries in an accounting system, such as invoices, materials requisitions and materials return notes.

principal Amount on which interest is charged to a borrower or paid to a lender.

prior-period adjustment Credit or debit made to adjust retained earnings because of significant previous errors or changes in accounting practice.

private ledger Ledger that details private accounts, often linked to the general ledger via a control account.

private limited company Company whose shares are not available to the general public through the medium of a stock exchange, and whose members do not exceed 50 in number. *See also* ***public limited company (plc)***.

proceeds Revenue from a business activity, disposal of assets or issue of securities. Sometimes the term is taken as a synonym of ***profit***.

process Operation that is involved in the production of goods or services.

process costing Cost accounting method used for continuous production which is based on average costs (total costs divided by the number of units produced). It may be necessary to differentiate between main products, joint products and by-products.

produce Goods that are grown (agricultural produce), or to grow or manufacture such goods.

product Something that is produced, either in terms of goods or services or in terms of income.

product costs Direct costs and indirect costs (overhead) expressed as cost per unit of production.

production Broadly, the practice of manufacturing goods or providing services for sale. It may be measured in units of production, labour costs, or the time (machine or labour hours) taken to produce it.

production budget Alternative term for ***operating budget***.

production cost Alternative term for ***manufacturing cost***.

production cost account Temporary account in which production costs are recorded for a given period.

production cost of sales For a given period, the production cost of goods sold during that period, including cost of sales and manufacturing overhead. Opening and closing stocks and work in progress should be taken into account.

production cost variance In standard costing, the difference between the standard cost of actual production and the actual cost.

production method of depreciation Assignment of a depreciable life to an asset in terms of units of output or time actually in use (rather than in terms of elapsed time).

production overhead Alternative term for ***manufacturing overhead***.

production profit Also known as profit on manufacture, the margin (profit) that results when finished goods leave the factory at a price that is greater than their cost of production. There could, of course, be a production loss.

production-unit method *See* ***production method of depreciation***.

production volume Alternative term for ***denominator volume***.

production-volume ratio (PV ratio) *See* ***contribution margin***.

production-volume variance Alternative term for ***denominator variance***.

productive capacity Measure of how much an asset (such as a machine) produces, expressed in such terms as units per year. This should be borne in mind when estimating the replacement cost of such an asset.

productivity Output of any of the factors of production (land, labour and capital) per unit of input. It may be enhanced by the improvement of any one of the three factors, most usually by the introduction of new technology or an incentive scheme. Productivity of land is generally measured in output per acre or hectare, that of labour in output per working hour, and that of capital as a percentage per annum.

productivity variance Alternative term for ***overhead efficiency variance***.

profit At its most general, the surplus money, after all expenses have been met, generated by a company or enterprise in the course of one accounting period. *See* ***gross profit; net profit***.

profitability index (PI) Way of putting proposed projects in order of profitability by predicting standard cash flows. The ratio of total present values of cash flows to initial investment is determined for each project, and only those with a ratio of greater than one are considered.

profit and loss account (P & L) Annual summary of a company's financial operations, required by law to be submitted to the UK Registrar of Companies by every trading company over a certain size (*see* ***small company***). The profit and loss account has three sections: the trading account, the profit and loss account and the appropriation account. The profit and loss section takes the (gross) profit or loss figure from the trading account, and after accounting for income not concerned with trading and expenses such as those incurred in administration, deducts tax from the final net profit or loss figure.

profit and loss account reserve Reserve containing the balance of retained earnings that are to be carried forward to the next accounting period (or distributed in whole or in part to shareholders).

profit and loss appropriation account Account that details how a company's net profits have been allocated. *See* ***profit and loss account***.

profit and loss sharing ratio The part of net income (or loss) that is allocated to a partner in a partnership.

profit and loss statement *See* ***profit and loss account***.

profit centre Part of an organization that creates revenue and to which costs can be assigned. *See also* **cost centre**.

profit margin Sales less all expenses (outgoings), usually expressed as a percentage of net sales or as simple net profit. Company policy generally specifies some profit margin below which it would be hardly worthwhile producing goods. *See also* ***gross margin; net margin***.

profit maximization Principle in accounting that operations should be presented in such a way as to make net income as large as possible.

profit on manufacture Alternative term for ***production profit***.

profits available for distribution Alternative term for ***distributable income***.

profit sharing Distribution of some or all of a company's profits to its employees as a bonus. The distribution may be in the form of cash or shares.

profit-sharing ratio (PSR) Ratio in which an organization's profits (or losses) are shared, often specified in a partnership agreement.

profit variance In standard costing, a variance equal to the difference between the budgeted operating profit and the actual profit made.

profit-volume chart Also called a PV chart, a graph that shows the profits (or losses) that would be made at various levels of activity (such as production or sales). *See also* ***breakeven chart***.

profit-volume ratio *See* ***contribution margin***.

pro-forma financial statement Financial statement based on estimates, because it is prepared before the end of an accounting period. It is therefore a forecast, also known as a projected financial statement.

pro-forma invoice Type of invoice submitted before goods are despatched, used to confirm an order and advise of despatch.

pro-forma statement *See* ***pro-forma financial statement***.

programmed costs US term for a fixed cost that is not essential for an operation. *See* ***discretionary costs***.

progressive tax Tax that increases as its base (e.g., income) increases. *See also* ***regressive tax***.

progress payment *See* ***payment on account***.

projected financial statement Alternative term for a ***pro-forma financial statement***.

project finance Funds set aside by a company for a particular project.

promissory note Document that states that a person promises to pay a certain sum of money on a certain date. It is also known as a note of hand.

proof of journal Checking the accuracy of journal entries (by making sure that all debits equal all credits).

proper accounting records Requirement under the Companies Act that a company keeps accounting records that detail its transactions (and thus show its financial status at any time).

property tax Tax based on the value of property, such as council tax in the UK (which is paid by the occupant of the property, who is not necessarily the owner).

proportional consolidation In group accounts, a method of consolidation in which each subsidiary company contributes proportionately to the joint venture's revenue.

proprietary accounts In the USA, accounts that record transactions of government departments.

proprietary company (Pty) Name of a private limited company in Australia and South Africa (Pty is used in a similar way to Ltd in the UK).

proprietary view Way of regarding an accounting entity from the owners' (i.e., shareholders') point of view.

proprietor Owner of a business or property.

proprietorship theory Idea that a company's owners are separate from its organization as an accounting entity, as emphasized by the accounting equation: equities = assets – liabilities. *See also* ***entity theory***.

prorate To allocate proportionately.

provision Allowance for some eventuality, such as a sum written off to provide for depreciation of assets.

provision for bad debts Provision for debts (which have to be individually specified) that are not expected to be paid within an accounting period.

provision for doubtful debts *See* ***allowance for doubtful accounts***.

provision for depreciation Provision for loss in value of an asset. *See* ***depreciation***.

P

prudence concept Concept that calls for a cautious view in accounting, such as the exclusion on the balance sheet of money owed but not received, and the inclusion of all liabilities, whether or not they must be met immediately. It therefore postulates a worst-moment scenario. *See also* ***accounting concepts***.

PSR Abbreviation of ***profit-sharing ratio***.

Pty Abbreviation of ***proprietary company***.

public accountant In the USA, a term that is usually synonymous with ***certified public accountant* (CPA)**.

public accounting Accounting activity centred mainly on the ***attest function***, resulting in an auditor's report.

publicity costs Costs incurred by an organization's publicity (i.e., advertising) activities, including salaries of the publicity manager and his or her staff, costs of advertising and promotions, and other point-of-sale costs.

public limited company (plc) Sometimes also rendered as Plc or PLC, a company whose shares are available to the general public through a stock exchange and is registered as such in the UK under the Companies Act 1980. Its authorized share capital must be at least £50,000, of which at least 25% must be paid up. *See also* ***private limited company***.

published accounts Company's accounts published according to the terms of the Companies Act 1985, most commonly those of limited companies, issued for their shareholders and filed at Companies House. *See also* ***small company***.

puisne mortgage Mortgage that has not been protected by depositing the title deeds of the property concerned. The lender may instead register the property with the Land Register or the Land Charges Register; this ensures that any transaction concerning the property must have the approval of the lender.

purchase allowance Reduction in selling price, usually because the goods or service supplied were not exactly as ordered.

purchase day book Also termed purchases journal, the book of prime entry that records invoiced costs of purchases.

purchased goodwill Goodwill that is acquired when an entity is purchased (rather than being generated internally). *See* ***goodwill***.

purchase discount Reduction in purchase price given for cash payment or for prompt payment.

purchase method In the USA, accounting method for business combinations. The value of the acquired company's assets are added (at the price paid for them) to the acquiring company's assets. *See also* ***pooling of interest method***.

purchase order Document giving a seller the authorization to deliver goods or services, to be paid for later.

purchase requisition Document giving a company's purchasing department the authorization to purchase specified goods or services.

purchases account Account that details transactions involving the purchase of goods or services (for cash or on credit).

purchases budget Budget for a company's purchases in a given period, used by its purchasing department.

purchases invoice Invoice sent to a supplier by a purchaser, recorded in the buyer's purchase day book.

purchases journal Alternative term for ***purchase day book***.

purchases ledger Alternative term for ***creditors' ledger***.

purchases ledger control account Alternative term for ***creditors' ledger control account***.

purchases returns Goods that are returned to a supplier because they are faulty or not as ordered.

purchasing power Person's or company's ability to buy goods and services. An organization with high purchasing power (such as a supermarket chain) can often negotiate lower prices with suppliers.

push-down accounting US practice of including in the accounts of an acquired subsidiary goodwill and other fair value adjustments.

PV chart Abbreviation of ***profit-volume chart***.

PV ratio Abbreviation of profit-volume ratio; *see* ***contribution margin***.

pyramid selling Practice of selling distributorships, or the right to sell distributorships. The pyramid seller makes his or her profit from the sale of ***franchises*** and leaves the franchisee to dispose of the goods. In a typical system, each franchisee must guarantee to purchase a certain quantity of goods, which he or she then disposes of by recruiting distributors. Those at the bottom of the pyramid usually sell to family and friends.

Q

qualified report Also termed a qualified audit report or qualified opinion, an auditor's report in which he or she qualifies the financial statements (because he or she does not sanction the way in which some matters are treated or because the scope of the audit has been limited for some reason).

qualifying loss Trading loss that arises because of corporation tax calculations.

qualitative factor Significant factor that cannot be precisely calculated in cash terms.

quality of earnings Extent to which a company's net profit gives an accurate reflection of its actual performance.

quantitative budget Budget that deals with non-financial factors in budgetary control (such as the amount of labour required or the number of units to be manufactured).

quantity discount Also termed quantity rebate, a reduction in purchase price granted because of the large amount of goods or services being purchased. *See* ***discount***.

quantity variance In standard costing, the actual amount of materials used less the standard quantity that should be used, multiplied by the standard price per unit.

quantum meruit If a supplier completes only part of the work he or she has been contracted to do, the supplier may in some cases claim payment in proportion to the work completed, known as payment quantum meruit (as much as he has earned).

quarterly report In the USA, a financial report that a company issues every three months.

quick assets Alternative term for ***liquid assets***.

quick ratio Alternative term for ***acid-test ratio***.

quote sheet In the USA, an analysis of costs that a company employs when deciding on a selling price for goods or services.

R

rateable value Value of a property for the purpose of calculating ***rates***, based on th estimated amount of rent the property would fetch (the annual value) on the open market and with vacant possession.

rate of interest *See* ***interest***.

rate of return Amount of money made on an investment (in the form of interest or dividend), normally expressed as a percentage of the amount invested. The revenue a company receives for investing resources in some commercial activity is also known as its rate of return.

rate of return pricing Using a required ***rate of return*** as a method of setting the selling price of a product.

rate of turnover Usually annual frequency at which a company asset or investment is turned over. For example, the ratio of sales revenue to the average value of stock gives the stock turnover figure.

rate per direct labour hour In absorption costing, the budgeted manufacturing overhead divided by the budgeted direct labour hours. It is a way of absorbing the manufacturing overhead into the cost units outputted.

rate per machine hour In absorption costing, the budgeted manufacturing overhead divided by the budgeted machine hours. It is a way of absorbing the manufacturing overhead into the cost units outputted.

rate per standard hour In absorption costing, the budgeted manufacturing overhead divided by the budgeted standard hours. It is a way of absorbing the manufacturing overhead into the cost units outputted.

rate per unit In absorption costing, the budgeted manufacturing overhead divided by the budgeted units. It is a way of absorbing the manufacturing overhead into the cost units outputted.

rates In the UK, a local government tax levied on householders and occupiers of commercial premises to pay for local works and services, expressed as a certain amount in the pound of ***rateable value***. For private property, rates have been replaced by ***council tax***, which is payable by the occupant.

rate variance Alternative term for price variance (of direct labour costs). It equals the difference between actual wages paid and the standard rate, multiplied by the total actual hours of direct labour employed.

ratio Result of dividing one number into another; a way of comparing quantities using proportions. *See* ***financial ratio***.

ratio analysis Using ***financial ratios*** to evaluate a company's performance.

raw material Any material purchased for and employed directly in a production process. Raw materials, such as chemicals, metal sheet and timber, are generally at a low level of finish compared to the manufactured product that results from their use.

raw material stock Inventory of raw materials, regarded as current assets on a balance sheet.

real accounts On a book-keeping ledger, the records of assets and capital. *See also* ***nominal accounts***.

real interest rate Actual interest rate minus current inflation rate, a more accurate indicator of the likely yield of an investment.

realizable account Also termed realization account, an account opened when a company is being would up and its assets are being realized in order to pay creditors, or a partnership is being dissolved. Proceeds from the sale of assets are placed in the realizable account.

realizable assets Alternative term for ***liquid assets***.

realizable value Amount that can be obtained by selling an asset; market value.

realization Selling of assets for cash.

realization account Alternative term for ***realizable account***.

realization convention In historical accounting, the practice of not recording changes in the value of assets and liabilities as gains or losses until assets have been sold and liabilities actually paid.

realize To sell assets for cash.

realized profit Profit that accrues when a transaction has been completed, usually the sale of goods or services, although the money has not necessarily been received (goods may be sold on credit, for example).

realized loss Loss that occurs when a transaction has been completed, usually the sale of goods or services, although the money has not necessarily been received (goods may be sold on credit, for example).

reallocation Also termed reapportionment, the allocation of the expense of running a service department to various production departments in proportion to the benefit they receive.

real rate of interest *See* ***real interest rate***.

real terms Value of goods or services arrived at by allowing for current price level fluctuations. *See* ***real value***.

real terms accounting Accounting system that estimates the effects of changing prices on a company's capital to discover whether value is being maintained in ***real terms***.

real value Value of something when compared to fluctuations in price indexes, as occur during times of inflation or deflation. For example, the real value of a 10% wage increase at a time of 5% inflation is only 5%, because the cash represented by the 10% increase will purchase only 5% more goods.

reapportionment Alternative term for ***reallocation***.

rearrangement costs Costs to a company of re-installing assets at a different location. They are usually accounted for in the same way as the original installation cost.

rebate Sum of money returned to a payer because he or she has paid too much. The term is also used as a synonym of ***discount***.

receipt Document stating that money has been paid or goods have been received. The acquisition of money is also termed the receipt of money; such acquisitions are called receipts (as opposed to expenditure).

receipts and payments basis Accounting basis in which accounts are drawn in terms of cash actually received or paid (as opposed to the ***accruals concept***).

receivables Any collectibles, whether or not they are currently due, such as claims for goods, services or money.

receivables turnover Also called accounts receivable turnover, for a given accounting period a financial ratio equal to net sales on account divided by average net accounts receivable.

receiver Official into whose hands a company in financial difficulties is placed to ensure that, as far as possible, its creditors are paid.

receivership State of a company when a ***receiver*** is called in.

reciprocal costs Costs allocated from a service cost centre to a production cost centre for services received. As a result, some costs of the production cost centre should be reciprocally allocated to the service cost centre.

reciprocal transfer *See* ***exchange***.

recognition Entering of an accounting item (transaction) into a company's financial statements (its 'books').

recognize To enter a transaction into a company's accounts.

recognized professional body (RPB) Professional body, recognized in the UK by the Securities and Investment Board, whose members can be authorized to carry out investment business as long as it does not constitute their main activity.

recognized supervisory body Organization, recognized in the UK by the Secretary of State for Trade and Industry, that supervises and controls auditors who carry out statutory audits.

recommended retail price (RRP) Price at which a manufacturer suggests his or her goods should be retailed. The RRP is often specified on the packaging to indicate to customers that the retailer is not overcharging and to allow a comparison to be made between the prices of competing brands.

reconciliation Calculation that demonstrates how one figure (such as a balance) is derived from another or others. *See*, e.g., ***bank reconciliation***.

recourse agreement In hire purchase transactions, an agreement that enables the seller to repossess the goods in the event of the purchaser being unable to make the payments required.

recoverable advance corporation tax Advance corporation tax that has already been paid but which can be set off against the current year's liability for gross corporation tax.

recoverable amount For an asset, its value in use or its net realizable value, whichever is the greater.

recovered overhead Alternative term for ***absorbed overhead***.

recovery rate Alternative term for ***absorption rate***.

red-circle rate Colloquial US term for a rate of pay that is higher than usual for the job undertaken.

reducing-balance depreciation Alternative term for ***decreasing-balance depreciation***.

refinancing Taking out a loan to pay back other borrowing. It is also termed refunding in the USA.

refunding US term for ***refinancing***.

register Collection of data, usually in alphabetical or in chronological order.

registered auditor Auditor who has been approved by EU authorities to carry out statutory audits (in accordance with the ***eighth directive***). In the UK, such approval may be given by a ***recognized supervisory body***.

registered book-keeper Member of the ***International Association of Book-keepers***.

registration for value added tax Requirement for a UK retailer who, broadly, sells more than £51,000 worth of taxable supplies (goods and services) per year to register with the Board of Customs and Excise and to charge (and remit) ***value added tax*** (VAT) on such goods and services.

regression analysis Measurement of the average change in one variable quantity resulting from unit increase in one or more other variable quantities.

regressive tax Tax that decreases as its base (e.g., income) increases. *See also* ***progressive tax***.

regulated loan Loan of £15,000 or less, regulated in the UK by the Consumer Credit Act 1974, that is not exempt under the Finance Act 1974 (which exempted loans for the alteration, improvement, purchase or repair of private dwellings).

reinvested earnings Alternative term for ***retained earnings***.

reinvestment rate In capital budgeting, the rate of investment of cash revenues accruing from a project before it is completed.

related parties Two or more parties who, during a financial period, are under common outside control or one party subordinates its separate interests because of outside control, or where one party influences financial policies of the other, or one party has control (direct or indirect) of the other.

related party transactions Transactions (such as performance of services or transfer of assets or liabilities) between related partics, whether or not they are charged for, which should be disclosed in the companies' annual accounts.

relative sales value method Method of allocating costs between joint products in proportion to their net realizable value.

relevant accounts Accounts that should be used to decide the amount of a company's distributable profit; the company's most recent audited accounts.

relevant cost Expenses that will change if a proposed decision is taken, also called an incremental cost.

relevant income Revenue that will change if a proposed decision is taken.

relevant range Activity levels between which cost functions are linear (and ***breakeven charts*** remain valid).

relevant revenue Alternative term for ***relevant income***.

remittance advice Document, accompanying a payment, that states why the payment is being made (it may, for example, refer to the number of the invoice that resulted in the payment).

remuneration Pay, such as a salary or a fee for professional services.

remuneration committee Committee of non-executive directors that decides a company's policy on the payment of executive directors, as recommended by the ***Greenbury Report***.

reorder level Lowest level of stock that can be held before more stock must be ordered.

reorganization Major restructuring of a company's capital, generally accompanied by changes in the rights and interests of shareholders.

reorganization costs Costs of restructuring a business, generally shown as a separate item on a company's profit and loss account.

repackaged perpetual debt Type of ***perpetual debt*** that has a high interest rate for several years before carrying little or no interest (and therefore having little or no value). It is generally transferred to a cooperative third party and then redeemed for a token amount.

repayment mortgage Mortgage in which repayments consist of interest payments and contributions towards the repayment of capital.

repair *See* ***repairs and maintenance***.

repairs and maintenance Costs of restoring and maintaining the service potential of an asset after prolonged use or damage. It is regarded as an expense (unlike improvements, which are generally regarded as capital expenditure).

replacement cost For a given asset, the current market price of another similar asset.

replacement cost accounting Type of ***current cost accounting*** in which assets are accounted for at their replacement cost (rather than historical cost).

replacement of business asset relief Also called roll-over relief, a form of relief from capital gains tax on gains made on the disposal of assets. If the gains are all reinvested in new business assets, no tax is payable.

replacement system of depreciation Method of depreciating an asset in which no depreciation is recorded during its service life, but when it is replaced the cost of its replacement is debited (less any residual salvage value of the old asset).

report and accounts *See* ***annual accounts***.

reporting accountants Accountants who comment on the financial information in the prospectus of a company proposing to issue shares.

reporting partner Partner in a firm of auditors who signs and dates an audit report after its approval by a company's directors.

report form Form of balance sheet on which assets less liabilities are shown as one total and the make-up of owner's equity is given as another (but also the same) total.

report of the auditor *See* ***auditor's report***.

repressed inflation *See* ***suppressed inflation***.

reproduction cost Acquisition cost of an asset that is the same in all physical respects as another for which a current value is required.

repurchase of own debt Method by means of which a company buys back its own debt for a different amount from the balance-sheet liability. The difference is recorded in the profit and loss account.

requisition Written request or order, such as one for items from the stores.

required rate of return Minimum ***rate of return*** that is needed in order to justify a company investment (i.e., for it to be profitable).

resale price maintenance Practice by means of which a supplier refuses to sell goods to a retailer unless the retailer agrees to sell them at a certain price, or above a minimum price. Resale price maintenance may be applied to prevent retailers from using a product as a ***loss leader***. It is allowable in the UK under the Resale Prices Act 1976 if the supplier can prove that it is in the interests of the consumer, as in the case of books and some pharmaceutical products.

resale value Alternative term for net realizable value or exit value (of an asset); market value.

reserve Part of a company's undistributed capital (excluding share capital) resulting from retained profits or the issue of shares at above nominal value.

reserve accounting Allowable transfer of items into reserves without their having passed through the profit and loss account (perhaps because of ***prior-period adjustments***).

reserve capital Also termed reserve liability, a part of a company's capital deemed not capable of being called up unless the company is would up.

reserve for bad debts Money put aside by a company against the possibility of unpaid debts (i.e., bad or doubtful debts).

reserve for obsolescence Money put aside to cushion a company against the possibility of its ***fixed assets*** becoming obsolescent or uneconomic.

reserve liability Alternative term for ***reserve capital***.

residual income (RI) Also called residual return, the net income generated by a subsidiary company or division after having paid a percentage return for the book value of the assets it controls.

residual interest Owners' equity in a company's assets after deduction of liabilities and any other higher priority claims.

residual return Alternative term for ***residual income***.

residual value *See* ***disposal value***.

responsibility accounting Method of accounting in which each unit is made a profit centre (i.e., each unit's manager is responsible for its expenses and revenues).

responsibility centre Alternative term for a profit centre in ***responsibility accounting***.

restricted assets In the USA, government resources that legal requirements or contractual terms restrict to specific purposes.

restricted retained earnings Part of retained earnings not legally available for paying dividends. *See* ***reserve capital***.

restrictive practice Agreement made between two companies that aims to make restrictions regarding the supply of their goods, on such things as price, quantities, processes, geographical area, and so on. On the whole, restrictive practices are assumed by the law to be against the general public interest.

retail price Price at which goods or services are actually sold through a retailer.

Retail Price Index (RPI) Analysis of trends in UK retail prices, expressed as an index number and used to evaluate changes in retail prices with reference to inflation. It is issued by the Central Statistical Office and is expressed as a percentage related to a base year, arbitrarily assigned the index 100. A similar index in the USA is known as the Consumer Price Index.

retained earnings That part of a company's post-tax earnings not distributed to shareholders, and thus retained by the company to finance its day-to-day activities and any future expansion. Retained earnings are added to ***reserves*** and thus appear on the company's balance sheet. They are also called retentions, retained income, retained profits or ploughed-back profits.

retained income Alternative term for ***retained earnings***.

retained profits Alternative term for ***retained earnings***.

retentions Alternative term for ***retained earnings***.

retirement method of depreciation Method of depreciating an asset in which no depreciation is recorded during its service life, but when it is retired from service its cost is debited (less any residual salvage value of the old asset).

retirement relief Relief of capital gains tax available in the UK on the gain resulting from the retirement of a business asset. It is to be phased out by 6 April 2003.

return Profits and income from transactions or investments. A return may also be a document sent to an authority (such as a census return or tax return).

return on assets Profit for a financial period expressed as a percentage of a company's assets.

return on capital employed (ROCE) Measure of how well a company's capital is used, equal to 100 times the profit (before tax and interest) divided by the average capital used.

return on investment (ROI) Measure of a company's performance, equal to 100 times the profit (before tax and interest) divided by the average total assets.

return period Three-monthly company accounting period for advance corporation tax and income tax, ending 31 March, 30 June, 30 September and 31 December.

returns inwards Also called sales returns, goods returned by customers to a supplier, usually because they are unsatisfactory in some way.

returns inwards book Also called sales returns book, a book of prime entry in which returns of goods sold are recorded.

returns outwards Goods returned by a company to its suppliers, usually because they are unsatisfactory in some way.

returns outwards book Book of prime entry in which returns of goods to suppliers are recorded.

revaluation Practice by means of which a company puts a new value on its fixes assets, because nominal values and real values of such assets as property and machines have changed significantly.

revaluation account Account in which historical values and current values (revaluations) of assets and liabilities are recorded after a partner enters or leaves a partnership. The resulting profit or loss is shared among the partners (in the ***profit-sharing ratio***).

revaluation method Method of calculating ***depreciation*** on a fixed asset. The asset is revalued annually, and any loss written off as depreciation (charged against the profit and loss account).

revaluation of assets *See* ***revaluation***.

revaluation reserve Reserve fund raised by a company by revaluing assets (at market price or replacement cost). Funds can also be raised by issuing shares at a premium above their par value.

revaluation reserve account *See* ***asset revaluation reserve***.

revenue Money received from any transaction or sale (including interest on investments); income. *The* Revenue is short for ***Inland Revenue***.

revenue account Accounts of a business that state the amount of money received from sales, commissions, and so on.

revenue centre Responsibility centre within a company whose manager controls only revenues (*see* ***responsibility accounting***).

revenue-cost graph Alternative name for a ***breakeven chart***.

revenue expenditure Expense written off to the profit and loss account in the period in which it occurs, as opposed to ***capital expenditure*** (to acquire an asset or pay a liability).

revenue function Equation used for presenting income graphically. An example is $y = bx$, where y is total revenue, b is the selling price (per unit of sales) and x is the number of units sold.

revenue received in advance Alternative term for ***advance*** (from customers).

revenue recognition Recording revenue in the correct financial period, often difficult with some complex transactions but usually taken to date from when the buyer assumes ownership of the item sold.

revenue reserve Distributable reserve (as opposed to a capital reserve).

revenue transaction Transaction written off to the profit and loss account in the period in which it occurs.

reversal entry Entry in an account in which all credits and debits are equal to the respective debits and credits from another entry, often made on the first day of an accounting period to reverse an adjusting entry made previously.

revision variance Alternative term for ***planning variance***.

revolving fund Fund that is automatically renewed at the start of each period (or as soon as it is depleted, such as a ***petty cash*** fund).

RI Abbreviation of ***residual income***.

risk Measure of the unpredictability or uncertainty of future events. In finance it can be taken as the amount one potentially stands to lose by a transaction, the probabilities of each possible outcome being known. For example, a high-risk investment can be expected to yield higher interest rates than a low-risk investment.

risk analysis Analysis of potential gains or losses from a financial transaction, such as an investment. Where there is a range of possible outcomes, their respective probabilities can be estimated.

risk-based audit Method that uses the results of assessing levels of the risk of errors (in a company's accounting system) to carry out audit tests.

risk capital Capital invested in a company, or security, that presents a risk (i.e., the probability of loss or, indeed, gain). The term is also used as an alternative to ***venture capital***.

risk management Measures adopted to minimize financial risk, such as hedging, insurance or spreading the risk.

risk premium In the USA, extra money paid to a worker (by way of a bonus) for tasking part in activities that are more risky than usual. In the UK it may be called danger money.

ROCE Abbreviation of ***return on capital employed***.

ROI Abbreviation of ***return on investment***.

rolling budget Budget that is automatically updated by adding on a further period (and dropping an equivalent period from the beginning of the budget).

roll-over relief Alternative term for ***replacement of business asset relief***.

RPB Abbreviation of ***recognized professional body***.

RPI Abbreviation of ***Retail Price Index***.

RRP Abbreviation of ***recommended retail price***.

ruling an account Method of summarizing a series of account entries, calculating a new balance, and drawing double lines beneath it.

running costs Also called running expenses, direct expenses or variable costs, the costs incurred in the day-to-day running of a business and which vary with the quantity of output. They include costs incurred in the purchase of the factors of production (such as raw materials and labour) and in the marketing, advertising and distribution of goods.

running expenses Alternative term for ***running costs***.

S

safety stock Stock level in stores that is sufficient to meet an unexpected increased demand or cope with an unexpected difficulty with supply.

salary Money paid to an employee, normally expressed as so much per year (or per annum) but usually paid by cheque or directly into the employee's bank account on a monthly basis. In some professions, a salary is referred to as a stipend. *See also* ***wage***.

sale Formally, the act of transferring goods or services from one person to another, accompanied by the exchange of money or by some sort of credit arrangement.

sale and leaseback Sale of property in which the buyer agrees to lease it back to its original owner. In this way, the seller is able to turn the property into liquid capital while at the same time remaining at the same location.

sale and purchase agreement Sale of an asset in which the seller is able to repurchase it under certain conditions. It is thus tantamount to a secured loan.

sale or return Agreement in which a distributor or retailer takes goods from a manufacturer or wholesaler on the understanding that he or she may return them if they are not sold within a specified period of time. Generally the goods are initially obtained on credit.

sales Colloquial name for the department within a company that deals with the sale of goods or services. An alternative definition makes sales an abbreviation of ***sales revenue***.

sales account Account that details cash and credit sales transactions.

sales allowance Reduction in invoice price for goods made usually because they are not exactly what was ordered. *See also* ***sales discount***.

sales budget Budget set for a company's sales function (usually specifying volume of and revenue from sales to be achieved in a given period).

sales credit note Note sent from a seller to a buyer to cancel (partly or in total) a charge that has already been invoiced. The credit thus granted can be offset against the cost of future purchases (and is therefore, from the seller's point of view, better than making a cash refund).

sales day book Also called sold day book or sales journal, the book of prime entry in which a company details invoices sent to customers (for goods or services supplied).

sales discount Discount on invoice price given by a seller of goods or services (usually in return for bulk purchases or prompt payment).

sales drive Effort to improve sales of and create demand for goods and services. Techniques include reducing prices, increasing the sales force or its commission, providing free samples and distributing point-of-sale advertising material.

sales forecast Estimate of future sales in terms of volume and, therefore, revenue. It takes into account past and predicted economic conditions.

sales function Department within a company that deals with the sale of its goods and services, often known colloquially as 'sales'.

sales invoice Document sent to a buyer by the a seller of goods of services (and often accompanying them) detailing the price and sometimes additional aspects such as discounts available, credit limits, date that payment is due, and so on.

sales journal Alternative name for ***sales day book***.

sales ledger Alternative name for ***debtors' ledger***.

sales ledger control account Alternative name for ***debtors' ledger control account***.

sales margin mix variance In standard costing, the difference valued at the standard margin between the sales volume of the actual mix (by product) and the sales volume of the budgeted mix. It is also called the sales mix profit variance.

sales margin price variance In standard costing, the difference between sales revenue and the budgeted sales volume (or the sales volume at standard selling price). It is also called the sales price variance.

sales margin volume variance In standard costing, the difference between the number of units sold and the budgeted number, at the standard profit margin. It is also called the sales volume variance.

sales mix Relative proportions of specific products in a mixture of products on sale.

sales mix profit variance Alternative term for ***sales margin mix variance***.

sales returns Alternative name for ***returns inwards***.

sales returns book Alternative name for ***returns inwards book***.

sales revenue Income from selling goods or services.

sales tax Tax imposed on goods or services at the point of sale, such as value added tax (VAT) in the UK.

sales value In process costing, a way of allocating joint costs among joint products. The costs of the independent production processes are deducted from the sales revenue of each product, resulting in a sales value for each at the ***separation point***. The joint costs are then allocated in proportion to each product's sales value.

sales volume Number of units of each good or service sold.

sales volume variance Alternative term for ***sales margin volume variance***.

salvage value Also called scrap value, the value of an asset at the end of its useful life (less disposal costs); ***net realizable value***.

Sandilands Committee Committee set up by the UK government in 1975 under the chairmanship of Sir Francis Sandilands. It was charged with recommending the best way to acknowledge the effects of inflation in company accounts, and ultimately recommended current cost accounting (as opposed to current purchasing power accounting).

SAS Abbreviation of ***Statement of Auditing Standards***.

SCARF Abbreviation of ***systems control and review file***.

schedule In US usage, a set of calculations that support how figures have been arrived at in a financial statement.

scorekeeping In management accounting, the monitoring of and reporting on staff (especially managers') performance.

scrap Waste material resulting from a production process, or the remains of an asset at the end of its useful life. Both may have a ***salvage value***.

scrap value Alternative name for ***salvage value***.

SEC Abbreviation of ***Securities and Exchange Commission***.

secondary auditor Auditor of a subsidiary company (and not also of the holding company). *See also* ***primary auditor***.

secondary production Production of goods that are manufactured, as opposed to the production of raw materials or foodstuffs (which are termed primary production).

second mortgage Additional mortgage on a property that is already mortgaged, granted only if the property has sufficient value to act as security for both loans.

secret profit Profit made by somebody by virtue of his or her employment by somebody else but not disclosed to the employer (such as a profit made by an agent who is also being paid commission). The activity is usually in breach of a contract and may result in a legal claim for damages.

secret reserve Alternative term for ***hidden reserve***.

secured creditor Creditor (such as a bank) that has a legal charge on one of the debtor's assets.

secured liability Debt in which the lender is safeguarded because the borrower has put up sufficient assets as security in the event of non-payment.

Securities and Exchange Commission (SEC) Government organization founded in 1934 that regulated the securities market (brokers and stock exchanges) in the USA. It also controls auditing practices and the financial reporting of companies.

Securities and Investment Board (SIB) UK financial watchdog, set up in 1986 by the Department of Trade and Industry to oversee the UK's deregulated financial markets.

securitization Situation in which an originator sells a package of assets to an issuer, so-called because he or she finances the purchase by issuing loan notes. Where the originator is a company, securitization may be a form of off-balance sheet finance.

security Anything (usually property) pledged as collateral against a loan, or the document that sets out the terms of such collateral. A security is also any financial instrument that is traded on a stock exchange and that yields an income. It represents a loan that will be repaid at some time in the future. Such securities include bills of exchange, bonds, debentures, gilt-edged securities, options, shares, stocks and unit trusts (but not insurance policies).

seed capital Also called seed money, capital put up to determine whether a proposed project is viable; ***venture capital*** lent to a very young company.

seed money *See* ***seed capital***.

segment Component of a business entity that has its own main activity or group of customers. It may be a subsidiary of a holding company, or a division or department within a single company.

segmental reporting Separation in a company's annual report and accounts of the results of its individual ***segments***, or the reporting of the performance of individual segments in management accounting.

segment margin Margin contributed by each ***segment*** of a company, less separable fixed costs.

segment reporting *See* ***segmental reporting***.

self-assessment Scheme introduced in 1996 (for the year to 5 April 1997) by the UK Inland Revenue that makes a taxpayer responsible for calculating his or her own liability for income tax. The calculation can, however, be delegated to the Revenue. After 1 July 1999 a similar scheme was introduced for companies.

self-balancing ledger Ledger with equal debits and credits, such as a personal ledger containing a control account.

Self-Regulating Organization (SRO) In the UK, a non-governmental organization that governs a particular area of business activity, laying down codes of practice and protecting consumers and investors. Five SROs were originally set up under the Financial Serrvices Act 1986 and recognized by the Securities and Investment Board; by 2000 there were only three.

self supply Value added tax (VAT) levied on a new commercial building used for an exempt purpose. The building costs and land attract output tax, but input tax is allowed on the building costs.

selling and administrative expenses Broad term for expenses that are not attributable to actual production.

selling costs Also known as selling overhead, the costs of a company's selling activities (including advertising, commissions and salaries).

selling overhead Alternative term for ***selling costs***.

selling price variance Alternative term for ***sales margin price variance***.

semi-fixed costs Also termed stepped costs, costs that increase step-wise with increasing activity. For example, an extra member of staff may be required each time production exceeds a certain level, and the labour cost on that job becomes a semi-fixed cost.

semi-variable costs Costs that increase in a linear manner, over and above an initial fixed cost, with increasing activity. Thus the fixed cost remains even when activity is zero.

senior debt Oldest existing debt owed by a person or company, hence the debt that should be paid first in normal circumstances.

sensitivity analysis Estimation of how predicted outcomes might be affected by changes in factors that determine those outcomes; i.e., how sensitive the outcomes are likely to be to those changes.

separate-entry concept Accounting concept that the business of an organization should be described in its financial statements as if it were totally separate from its owners.

separation point In a process that produces by-products or joint products, the stage at which the products separate, to be further processed independently. It is also called the split-off point.

service Something provided, usually for a fee, that may not be classed as manufacturing or production in any form (such as accountancy services, legal advice, brokerage, and so on).

service cost centre Alternative term for ***indirect cost centre***.

service department Alternative term for ***indirect cost centre***.

service life Expected time period during which an asset is usable.

service industry Businesses engaged in the service, or tertiary, sector, such as a shop or hairdressing business.

service potential Future benefits that should accrue from an asset.

services *See* ***service***.

servicing a debt Paying interest on a debt.

servicing a loan Paying interest on a loan.

set-off In accounting, two parties that have an indebtedness to each other may set off both debts against each other by assuming that one debt has paid off the other and *vice versa*. Such an arrangement is termed a set-off.

settlement Act of paying in full for goods or services received, or of repaying a debt or loan.

settlement discount Discount offered for early or prompt settlement of an account.

set-up Describing the time or costs involved in preparing a production process for doing its job.

set-up time *See* ***set-up***.

Seventh Directive Directive of the European Community (now European Union) of 1983 concerning the preparation of consolidated financial statements by groups and holding companies. It was incorporated in the UK Companies Act 1989.

SFAC Abbreviation of ***Statement of Financial Accounting Concepts***.

SFAS Abbreviation of ***Statement of Financial Accounting Standards***.

severance pay Sum of money given to an employee when he or she is made redundant.

shell company Company that does not produce anything in the usual sense, but exists only in name. Shell companies may be set up and sold to people who are unfamiliar with the procedure for doing this, or may be the remnants of a defunct company that has been sold on to somebody else. They may also be set up for use at some future time, or to operate as the holder of shares. *See also* ***paper company***.

short credit Loan that must be repaid over a short timescale, usually taken in the UK to be three months or less, although in the USA a period of up to a year may be considered to be short-term (or near-term).

short-form audit report In the USA, an audit report prepared according to official short-form reporting requirements.

short-run performance margin Margin contributed by each segment of a company, less certain separable costs.

short-term *See* ***short credit***.

short-term capital Loan capital lent in the short term, i.e., for less than five years in the UK.

short-term interest rate Interest rate on a short-term loan. *See* ***short credit***.

short-termism Policy of maximizing current profits rather than investing in future developments.

shrinkage Mainly in retailing, a euphemism for theft (of goods or stock) by employees. For some products, genuine shrinkage may occur because of evaporation.

SIAS Abbreviation of ***Statement of Internal Auditing Standards***.

SIB Abbreviation of ***Securities and Investment Board***.

simple interest Rate of interest calculated by keeping interest that has already accrued separate from the capital sum. Thus, when calculating the next interest payment, the capital sum only (excluding the interest already accrued) enters the calculation. In mathematical terms, simple interest equals $Atr/100$, where A is the amount invested or borrowed, t is the time in years and r is the interest rate as a percentage per annum. *See also* ***compound interest***.

simplified financial statements Simplified form of a company's annual report and accounts, meant for people without in-depth financial experience. *See also* ***employee report***.

SIN Abbreviation of ***stores issue note***.

single-entry accounting *See* ***single-entry book-keeping***.

single-entry book-keeping Method of book-keeping in which only one aspect of a transaction (i.e., either a debit or a credit) is recorded. It is not self-balancing, i.e., debits and credits are not kept equal and no journal entries are made.

single proprietorship US term for ***sole proprietorship***.

single-step income statement Statement that groups together and totals all revenues and then deducts all expenses (also grouped together), without any intermediate subtotals being shown.

sinking fund Sum of money set aside for a specific purpose and invested so that it provides the required amount at the right time. The fund's earnings are liable for tax.

skeleton account Another name for a ***T-account***.

skunk costs US term for costs that have already been ascribed to a project and cannot be clawed back if the project is aborted.

sleeping partner Partner who invests capital in a firm but takes no active part in its management. He or she does, however, remain liable for the partnership's debts.

slide US term for an accounting error caused by a book-keeper putting a decimal point in the wrong place.

slippage Underperformance of a start-up company, which may lead to the need for additional capital.

small company Company that meets various criteria and is thereby permitted to issue less detailed annual reports to shareholders and file abbreviated accounts with Companies House. Its turnover has to be less than £2.8 million, its balance-sheet total less than £1.4 million and its number of employees fewer than 50. If its turnover is less than £90,000 and balance-sheet total less than £1.4 million, it is exempt from a statutory audit of its accounts.

small companies relief *See **marginal relief**.*

soak-up method Alternative US term for ***equity method***.

social audit Audit of a company's impact on society.

socially responsible investment Alternative term for ***ethical investment***.

sold day book Alternative name for ***sales day book***.

sold ledger Alternative term for ***debtors' ledger***.

sole agency Agreement by which an agent represents a principal exclusively either in a certain capacity or in a certain geographical area.

sole practitioner *See **sole proprietorship**.*

sole proprietor *See **sole propritorship**.*

sole proprietorship Unincorporated business that is run by one person on his or her own. The sole proprietor of a professional practice (such as an accountant or solicitor) is known as a sole practitioner. The sole proprietor of another type of business is generally known as a sole trader.

sole trader *See **sole propritorship**.*

solicitor's accounts Accounts prepared by or for a solicitor (which have to conform to the Solicitors' Account Rules, particularly with regard to accounting for the practice's money separately from money held on behalf of clients).

Solomons Reports Reports concerning accountancy produced by Professor David Solomons. His *Prospectus for a Profession* of 1974 concerned the training of accountants, and *Guidelines for Financial Reporting Standards* of 1989 proposed a conceptual framework for financial accountancy.

solvency The state of a person or company that is cash positive and able to pay all bills as they fall due; i.e., its assets are more than its liabilities. The converse is insolvency.

solvent Describing a person or company in a state of ***solvency***.

SORP Abbreviation of ***Statement of Recommended Practice***.

sound value Mainly US term for replacement cost or fair market value of a fixed asset.

source and application of funds Company statement outlining how it has raised funds and used them in a particular period. *See also* ***cash-flow statement***.

source of funds Revenue from any transaction that contributes further working capital.

sources and uses statement US term for ***sources and application of funds***, formally called ***statement of changes in financial position*** in the USA.

special agent Agent with the authority to perform one particular activity on behalf of another. *See also* ***universal agent***.

special assessment In US government accounting, a levy made on property to pay for improvements that will not benefit the general public but only the owner of the property.

Special Commissioners Professional civil servants who hear appeals against assessments of capital gains tax, corporation tax or income tax. *See also* *General Commissioners*.

special journal Journal for recording frequently-occurring similar transactions, such as a cash payments journal or a sales journal.

specific order costing *See* ***job costing***.

special revenue debt In US government accounting, debt of a unit that has revenues from only specific sources (such as tolls for a road or bridge).

specific identification method Method of valuing existing stock (ending inventory) and cost of goods sold by counting how many units have been sold and totalling their actual costs.

specific price changes Changes in market prices of specified goods and services (as opposed to general changes in price levels).

specific price index Index that indicates the price of a particular good or service (relative to a base price), as opposed to a ***general price index***.

spending variance In standard costing, the price variance for variable overhead costs.

split-off point Alternative term for ***separation point***.

spoilage Also called waste, materials lost during a production process. Normal loss is an acceptable level of spoilage.

S

spreadsheet Table of numbers arranged in rows and columns. Paper spreadsheets, also called work sheets, provided a method of classifying accounting information in two ways (perhaps with rows labelled with various debits and columns labelled with credits). Manual methods have almost entirely been replaced by computerized spreadsheets, whose principal advantage is that they can immediately show the effects of changing a single entry, which is extremely useful in planning.

SRN Abbreviation of ***stores returns note***.

SRO Abbreviation of ***Self-Regulating Organization***.

SSAP Abbreviation of ***Statement of Standard Accounting Practice***.

stabilized accounting Method of accounting that makes adjustments for changes in price levels. *See* ***price-level accounting***.

stable monetary unit assumption Basis of ***historical cost accounting***.

standard absorption costing Method of costing finished products by totalling the standard costs allowed for the various factors of production (including overhead), and not by taking account of the actual costs incurred. *See* ***absorption costing***.

standard cash flow pattern In a discounted cash flow calculation, the usual situation where, after an initial cash outflow, there are regular inflows during the remainder of the project.

standard cost Predetermined cost (usually per unit) that is assigned to a product and should be attained. It is also termed target cost.

standard cost allowance In a standard costing system for variable costs, the expenditure allowed for bearing in mind the actual number of units produced.

standard costing Method of determining and controlling product costs by means of ***standard costs***, which are regularly compared with actual costs.

standard cost system Alternative US term for ***standard costing***.

standard direct costing Method of determining product cost by totalling the ***standard cost allowances*** for the factors of production (excluding fixed overhead).

standard direct labour cost In standard costing, a standard cost calculated from the standard time allowed and the standard direct labour rate.

standard direct labour rate In standard costing, a predetermined rate of pay for direct labour used to calculate standard direct labour costs.

standard direct materials cost In standard costing, a standard cost calculated from the standard quantity of materials allowed and the standard direct materials price for a given product.

standard direct materials price In standard costing, a predetermined price for direct materials used in calculating the standard direct materials cost.

standard fixed overhead cost In standard costing, a standard cost calculated using the standard time allowed and the standard fixed overhead absorption rate.

standard hour Amount of work that can normally be done or number of units that can normally be produced in an hour. It is a measure of production, used to calculate ***efficiency ratios***.

standard marginal costing In marginal costing, a method of determining and controlling product costs in which predetermined standard costs and income required are set and regularly compared with actual costs.

standard materials usage Predetermined quantity of materials to be used in producing something. In standard costing, the direct materials usage variance can be found by comparing the standard materials usage with the actual quantity used.

standard operating cost Sum of all the ***standard cost allowances*** for the actual quantity of production.

standard operating profit For a given operation, the budgeted revenue minus the standard operating cost.

standard overhead cost In standard costing, a standard cost for overhead (fixed, variable or both) calculated from the standard time allowed for a process and the standard overhead absorption rate.

standard price In standard costing, the predetermined unit price for labour or materials.

standard production cost In standard costing, production cost calculated from predetermined costs and performance levels.

standard purchase price In standard costing, a predetermined price set for direct materials for a given period. Direct materials price variances can be calculated by comparing this price with the actual prices paid.

standard quantity allowance In standard costing, the quantity of direct labour or direct materials that should be used in production if predetermined standards apply.

standard rate Rate of value added tax (VAT), since 1 April 1991 set at 17.5%, applied in the UK to all goods and services except for exempt supplies or zero-rated goods and services. The ***basic rate*** of income tax is also sometimes referred to as the standard rate.

standard rate of pay Predetermined rate of pay set for each job in a given period. In standard costing, direct labour rate of pay variances can be determined by comparing this rate with the actual rates paid.

standard selling price Predetermined selling price set for product in a given period. In standard costing, sales margin price variances can be determined by comparing this price with the actual prices obtained.

standard time In standard costing, the time allowed for a given production task, expressed as either the output achieved in standard hours or the standard time allowance.

standard variable overhead cost In standard costing, a standard cost calculated from the standard time allowed and the standard variable overhead absorption rate.

standby costs Costs that are still incurred even if business operations are completed shut down (such as rates and other property taxes).

start-up company Usually a new company that is beginning from scratch. It may need ***venture capital*** to help it on its way.

statement of account Document issued by a creditor (to a debtor) detailing transactions to date and any balance still due.

statement of affairs Type of ***statement of account*** that details a person's or company's financial position at a given time, particularly the assets and liabilities of a company in liquidation (or a person in bankruptcy).

Statement of Auditing Standards (SAS) Statement about auditing principles and procedures published by the Auditing Practices Board. In most of their activities, auditors have to comply with these statements.

statement of changes in financial position Term used in the USA for a statement concerning changes in a company's working capital during an accounting period. It is also known informally as a funds statement.

Statement of Financial Accounting Concepts (SFAC) Statement about basic accounting and reporting concepts issued in the USA by the *Financial Accounting Standards Board (FASB)*.

Statement of Financial Accounting Standards (SFAS) Statement about accounting and reporting requirements issued in the USA by the

Financial Accounting Standards Board (FASB).

statement of financial condition US synonym for ***balance sheet***.

statement of financial position US synonym for ***balance sheet***.

Statement of Principles Discussion paper abut financial reporting issued by the ***Accounting Standards Board (ASB)***.

statement of profit and loss US synonym for profit and loss account, also called an income statement.

Statement of Recommended Practice (SORP) Statement concerning accounting matters issued by the Accounting Standards Committee (now superseded by the Accounting Standards Board, which does not issue statements under this heading).

statement of retained earnings Financial statement that details changes in ***retained earnings*** (or retained income) during a given accounting period. It reconciles the opening and closing balances on the retained earnings account.

statement of retained income Alternative term for ***statement of retained earnings***.

statement of sources and applications of funds US synonym of ***statement of changes in financial position***. *See also* ***source and application of funds***.

Statement of Standard Accounting Practice (SSAP) Accounting standard drawn up by the Accounting Standards Committee. A total of 25 SSAPs have been issued since 1971, although some have been amended.

Statement on Auditing Statement about auditing practice, particularly of larger firms, issued by the ***Institute of Chartered Accountants***.

Statement on Internal Auditing Standards (SIAS) Statement issued by a committee of the USA-based ***Institute of Internal Auditors***.

state of nature *See* ***event***.

static budget Budget drawn up for a single level of activity and therefore not automatically adjusted when activity levels change. It is also called a fixed budget.

statute-barred debt Debt that may longer be called in because it has been outstanding for too long (more than six years in the UK, as defined by the Statute of Limitations Act 1939).

statutory accounts Legally required accounts, such as those made obligatory under the terms of the Companies Act.

statutory audit Company audit as required under the terms of the Companies Act. The auditor's report is presented to the members of the company at a general meeting. Small companies may be exempt from a statutory audit (*see* ***small company***).

statutory books Books of account that a company must keep under the terms of the Companies Act. *See* ***books of account***.

statutory company Company set up by the UK government (by Act of Parliament) to produce essential services such as the provision of power and water.

step costs US term for ***semi-fixed costs***.

step-down method Method of allocating the costs of a service department to other service departments within a company as well as to production departments. The other service departments then have their costs allocated in a similar way, except no costs are charged back to service departments whose costs have already been allocated. Eventually, in this way, all service costs are charged to production.

step-function costs Alternative term for stepped costs; *see* ***semi-fixed costs***.

stepped costs Alternative term form ***semi-fixed costs***.

step-variable costs US term for ***semi-fixed costs***.

stipend Alternative term for ***salary***.

stock The stock-in-trade of a company (synonymous with inventory), i.e., a collection of raw materials or goods held by a manufacturer, wholesaler, retailer or end-user, or any collection of company assets. The term also denotes a fixed-term security denominated in units of £1.00, or it means an ordinary share in a company (especially in US usage).

stock budget Budget that plans volumes and values of stock, work in progress and finished goods during a given period.

stock control Alternative term for ***inventory control***.

stock-in-trade Alternative term for ***stock***.

stock ledger Ledger that details changes in levels of stock (inventory), i.e., stock purchased, stock consumed and stock-in-hand.

stock out Describing a situation when a given item is out of stock (i.e., none is held in store).

stock reconciliation Purpose of ***stocktaking***.

stock record In inventory control, a record of changes in levels of stock (inventory), usually itemized in a ***stock ledger***.

stocks *See* ***stock***.

stocktaking Task of counting (and often valuing) the stock-in-trade of an organization, such as a manufacturing company, wholesaler, retailer or end-user. The stock valuation appears in a company's financial records at the end of an accounting period. Some organizations carry out ***continuous stocktaking***, often with the aid of a computer program.

stock turnover Alternative term for ***inventory turnover***.

stock valuation Alternative term for ***inventory valuation***. *See also* ***stocktaking***.

store card Alternative name for a ***bin card***.

stores Department of a company where stock (inventory) is kept; often there are separate stores for raw materials and finished goods. The stock itself is also sometimes known as stores.

stores issue note (SIN) Alternative term for ***materials requisition***.

stores oncost Additional expense that arises through storing goods, principally stock.

stores requisition Alternative term for ***materials requisition***.

stores returns note (SRN) Alternative term for ***materials returns note***.

straight-line depreciation Method of calculating the rate of ***depreciation*** of an asset. A fixed proportion of the total original value of the asset is written off in each accounting period, making allowance for its current resale value either as a useful asset or as scrap (salvage value). Thus the depreciation at any one time is the asset's original cost less net residual value, divided by its predicted lifetime (in years).

strategic management accounting Type of management accounting that uses financial information to make long-term planning decisions (as opposed to short-time adjustments to company policy).

subjective goodwill Company goodwill determined by taking the net present value of estimated future cash flow and deducting from it the present net tangible assets.

subject to Qualification on an auditor's report usually because there is a significant uncertainty in the accounts concerned. The report is therefore subject to any adjustments that have to be made.

subordinated debt Debt whose claim for repayment comes after (is junior to) claims of other debts. An unsecured creditor's debt is subordinated to those of secured creditors.

subordinated loan Loan that does not have repayment priority (*see **subordinated debt***).

subsequent events Alternative term for ***post-statement events***.

subsidiary Company that has more than 50% of its voting shares owned by another company (which is known as the parent or ***holding company***). *See also* ***consolidation***.

subsidiary ledger Ledger from which account totals are transferred to a controlling account in the general ledger.

subsidy Sum paid by the government to companies in certain industries to enable them to sell their goods or services at a price close to the prevailing market price. A subsidy is also used to provide financial support to a commercial or quasi-commercial activity that would otherwise not be viable in narrow profit-and-loss terms, usually in order to sustain broader economic or social benefits.

substance over form General accounting principle that transactions are accounted for in terms of their commercial reality (substance), not their legal form. ***Creative accounting***, for example, does not follow this principle.

substantive tests Tests carried out in an audit to check various aspects of a company's financial records and statements.

subsubsidiary Subsidiary company of a ***subsidiary***.

subvention In the UK, a payment made from one company to another (related) company in order to give a better picture of the group's performance. In the USA, a grant made by the government, a company or other institution to a non-profit making organization.

summary financial statement Shortened form of a company's report and accounts that, since 1 April 1990, may be sent to shareholders instead of the full report (as long as certain conditions are complied with).

sum-of-the-years'-digits depreciation (SYD) Method of calculating accelerated ***depreciation*** of an asset. The digits that make up the asset's estimated life are added together, to give the denominator of a fraction.

The numerator of this fraction for the first year is the lifetime, and this fraction is written off as depreciation. For the second year, the numerator is one less, and so on. For example, if an asset's estimated lifetime is 6 years, the sum of its digits is $6 + 5 + 4 + 3 + 2 + 1 = 21$. In the first year, 6/21 of the value is written off; in the second year, 5/21 of the value; in the third year, 4/21 of the value, and so on.

sundry expenses Small items of expenditure, not worth accounting for under other headings. *See also* ***petty cash***.

sunk cost Cost (usually of purchasing an asset) that has been incurred and can be accounted for as an asset even though its value is irrecoverable; for example, the costs of earthworks for a building project. In this sense it is a type of historical cost.

supplementary benefit Payment made by the UK government to somebody who is either out of work but does not qualify for unemployment benefit, or is on a very low wage.

supplementary statement Any additional, non-obligatory financial statement appended to a company's accounts.

supply To provide goods and services.

supply and demand Two market forces that in microeconomic theory determine the prices of goods, services or investment instruments. If supply is low and demand high, prices increase. Conversely, if demand is low and supply high, prices fall (unless price controls are in operation).

supply risk In limited recourse financing of a construction project, the risk that the materials required may not be available some time after the project has been started.

support cost centre Alternative term for ***indirect cost centre***.

suppressed inflation Inflationary trend that has been slowed down or completely halted, usually by extensive government intervention in the economy. It is also known as repressed inflation.

surety Alternative term for ***collateral***.

surplus Formerly used in the USA terms 'earned surplus' (meaning retained earnings), 'capital surplus' (meaning capital contributed in excess of par value) and 'surplus reserves' (meaning appropriated retained earnings), the word 'surplus' is no longer approved of in these expressions.

surplus advance corporation tax Advance corporation tax over the available maximum for set-off against gross corporation tax in the current accounting period.

surplus reserves *See* ***surplus***.

suspense account Temporary account that records part of a transaction before complete analysis of that transaction, or that records sums to correct errors.

sustainable income Part of distributable income that a company can expect to earn in the next accounting period if it continues at its present level of activity.

switch selling Salesperson's technique whereby, if a potential buyer resists a particular product, another (equally attractive) one is suddenly made available.

SWOT analysis Acronym of strengths, weaknesses, opportunities and threats, aspects that an organization should consider in analysing its present position and in planning for the future.

SYD Abbreviation of ***sum-of-the-years'-digits depreciation***.

synergy Additional benefits to be gained by the combination of hitherto separate activities. It is sometimes colloquially expressed as '2 + 2 = 5', and cited to justify the take-over or merger of companies with complementary or mutually reinforcing activities or resources.

systems-based audit Audit that tests the quality of a company's accounting system by studying that company's internal control system. *See also* ***risk-based audit***.

systems control and review file (SCARF) Computerized auditing system formed by additing a program or additional financial data to a company's existing computerized accounting system. The contents of the SCARF file can be changed or deleted only by the external auditors.

T

T-account Accounting form shaped like the capital letter T. The name of the account is written above the T, debits are written on the left-hand side and credits on the right-hand aside.

take back When a US company is sold, the take back is a situation in which the owner must accept payment in something other than cash.

take-home pay Wages or salary remaining after all deductions (such as income tax, national insurance in the UK or Social Security in the USA) have been made.

taking a bath US colloquialism for incurring a large loss.

tallyman Accountant who works for a bookmaker on a race course.

tangible assets Literally, assets that may be touched, such as buildings or stock. They may be contrasted with intangible (or invisible) assets, such as a company's goodwill or the expertise of its staff. *See also* ***fixed asset***.

tangibles Alternative term for ***tangible assets***.

taper relief Tax relief that can be set against any capital gain made by selling assets after 6 April 1998. Its amount depends on the kind of asset and how long it has been held.

TAR Abbreviation of ***throughput accounting ratio***.

tare When the weight of goods is being established, the tare is the weight allowed for the packaging. It is also the weight of a (goods) vehicle without fuel; its unladen weight.

target cost Alternative term for ***standard cost***.

target costing Predetermined cost ceiling that is assigned to a production process to make the product's selling price competitive.

target price Average price for commodities fixed by the Common Agricultural Policy of the EU and achieved by purchasing goods at the ***intervention price***.

target rate In capital budgeting, the lowest required rate of return or the budgeted rate of return.

tax Money paid to central or local government to finance its expenditure and implement its financial policy. Various kinds of taxes are collected by the Inland Revenue in the UK (the Internal Revenue Service in the USA), HM Customs and Excise (in which case the tax is known as ***duty***) and local government authorities. *See also* ***rates; value added tax (VAT)***.

tax abatement Reduction in the rate of tax. It should not be confused with a tax rebate.

taxable income Income on which taxes are levied. It is calculated by deducting personal allowances (and any other tax-deductible expenses) from gross income.

taxable person Individual or organization who, in the course of business, charges value added tax (VAT) on taxable supplies.

taxable supply Any goods or services that are not an exempt supply. They are subject to value added tax (VAT).

tax accountant Accountant who specializes in tax matters, including assisting clients to prepare tax returns.

tax allocation Splitting a charge to tax among various sources of income.

tax allowance Deduction from gross income to give taxable income.

tax and price index (TPI) Index introduced in 1979 to compare levels of taxation with retail prices and relate them to average wage levels. The TPI is used to calculate the real spending power of the nation.

tax assessment Calculation of a person's income tax liability made by the Inland Revenue. If actual income figures are not available it may be estimated.

taxation Imposition and subsequent collection of tax.

tax avoidance Legal avoidance of or reduction in income tax, achieved by arranging one's financial affairs so as to take advantage all possible concessions. Such a device is also termed a tax shelter in the USA. Tax avoidance should not be confused with tax evasion (which is illegal).

tax base Form of income upon which tax is calculated. For example, the tax base for income tax is a person's taxable income, for corporation tax a company's profits.

tax bracket The percentage of a person's income that he or she pays in tax depends on the level of income. Incomes are divided into brackets (ranges) for the purpose of calculating tax. The term is also applied to people in that bracket. *See* ***basic rate; higher-rate tax***.

tax code Code number issued by the Inland Revenue to take account of a UK taxpayer's personal allowance and any other allowance to which he or she is entitled. For people taxed at source (***pay-as-you-earn***) the employer uses the tax code to calculate the amount of income tax to deduct from wages or salary.

tax commissioners *See* ***General Commissioners; Special Commissioners***.

tax credit That part of a dividend payment on which a company has already paid tax, thus relieving the shareholder from the necessity of doing so.

tax concession Allowance made by the Inland Revenue to taxpayers in certain categories, which means that these people or companies pay less tax than they would otherwise be liable for. For example, tax concessions are often used by government to induce companies to relocate in areas of high unemployment.

tax-deductible Describing the amount that may be deducted from personal income or company profits to establish the tax liability.

tax deduction Money removed from a person's salary or wages to pay income tax. In the USA, however, the term means expenses that are deductible against tax.

tax deduction card In pay-as-you-earn (PAYE) income tax, a record of all deductions made by an employer at source, submitted for each employee to the Inland Revenue annually.

tax-effective Describing a reduction in tax by a method that is in accordance with tax law.

Taxes Management Act 1970 UK legislation concerning administration and collection of capital gains tax, corporation tax and income tax.

tax evasion Evasion of tax liabilities by providing false information to the Inland Revenue. It is a criminal offence in the UK. *See also* ***tax avoidance***.

tax exemption Not having to pay tax. In the USA, however, the term describes the proportion of income upon which tax is not payable.

tax exile Person who lives abroad in order to minimize liability for tax.

tax-free Describing any allowance, benefit or other income that is not subject to tax.

tax gap Difference between the amount somebody owes the Inland

Revenue (Internal Revenue Service in the USA) and the amount he or she actually pays.

tax haven Country (such as the Bahamas, the Cayman Islands, Liechtenstein and Monaco) that has liberal tax and banking regulations. In some instances it benefits companies to set up their registered offices in such a country, to avoid paying taxes in their own country.

tax holiday Period during which a start-up company need not pay taxes.

tax invoice With value added tax (VAT), a detailed invoice that one taxable person sends to another when the taxable supply is worth £100 or more.

tax loss Loss sustained by a person or business which may, once incurred, be offset against a demand for capital gains tax, corporation tax or income tax. Tax losses are frequently incurred deliberately in an attempt to reduce the real cost of paying taxes.

taxman Informal name for an Inspector of Taxes.

taxpayer identification number (TIN) In the USA, a nine-digit number with no alphabetic characters, usually the same as a person's Social Security number or employee identification number.

tax period Period of time for which a return for value added tax (VAT) applies (usually three months). The return should be sent to Customs and Excise within a month of the end of the period.

tax point Date on which goods or services are sent to a customer. It identifies the tax period in which value added tax (VAT) is accounted for.

tax rebate Repayment of tax that has already been paid (usually because it was assessed too high).

tax relief Concessions made to taxpayers in respect of certain liabilities (such as, at one time, mortgages).

tax return Document submitted to the Inland Revenue annually, stating a person's earnings and expenses for the year and used to calculate a person's tax liabilities. *See also **self-assessment**.*

tax shelter Investment instrument that does not attract tax. In the USA, the term is also used for ***tax avoidance***. *See also **tax haven**.*

tax shield US term for non-cash items charged against income, thereby 'shielding' that amount from tax. Depreciation is an example of a tax shield.

tax tables Tables used by employers to calculate the income tax payable by employees under the pay-as-you-earn (PAYE) method. The calculations are often computerized.

tax week Any whole week following 6 April, the start of the tax year (fiscal year).

tax year Another term for ***fiscal year***.

teaser Colloquial term for an initial low rate of interest on an adjustable-rate mortgage (ARM), which may seem very attractive at the time of the arrangement, but which inevitably rises.

technological risk In limited resource financing of a construction project, the risk that new equipment will not work properly.

teeming and lading UK term for what in the USA is usually called ***lapping***.

temporary accounts Also called nominal accounts, accounts that do not appear on a company's balance sheet, such as expenses and revenue accounts, production cost accounts and purchases-related accounts.

temporary difference Also called timing difference, a difference between taxable and pre-tax income, reported to a company's shareholders, that will be reversed in a later accounting period. It is recorded in a deferred income tax account.

temporary diminution in value Short-term reduction in an asset's value. No adjustment is made for it in historical cost accounting. *See also* ***permanent diminution in value***.

temporary employment Full- or part-time employment in the short term, sometimes with a specified time limit and often without a formal contract of employment.

temporary investment Investment in a security that is to be sold within a year, and therefore a current asset.

tender Generally, an offer to supply goods or services at a certain price and under certain conditions. A tender is usually submitted in response to an invitation to do so, normally in competition with other potential suppliers.

ten-year charge For certain discretionary trusts, inheritance tax charged every 10 years. It is set at 30% of the lifetime rate.

terminal-loss relief Relief for an organization's loss made in the last year of its existence. The loss can be set off against the previous three years' profits.

terminal value Alternative term for ***disposal value***.

term loan Fixed loan made for a specified number of years, unlike a demand loan which a borrower may be asked to repay at any time.

terms of sale Conditions that relate to the payment for goods or services. They may include a latest date for payment and discounts for prompt or cash payment.

test data Data used by an auditor to test a company's computerized accounting or auditing systems.

thin capitalization Situation in which, in the view of the tax authorities, a company's capital includes too much loan stock and too few shares.

three-column cash book Cash book that has, in addition to columns for income (receipts) and outgoings (payments made), a column for recording discounts received and allowed. *See also* ***two-column cash book***.

threshold company Company that has moved beyond the start-up stage and is moving towards becoming secure and more profitable.

threshold price Price fixed by the European Commission under the Common Agricultural Policy (CAP), below which the price of agricultural imports from non-member states is not allowed to fall.

throughput accounting Method of short-term decision making in which conversion costs are regarded as fixed and products assigned a rank if they involve a particular constraint or scarce resource. *See* ***throughput accounting ratio***.

throughput accounting ratio (TAR) In throughput accounting, the ratio of the sales price less material cost, divided by hours on a scarce resource, to the total factory cost divided by total hours of constraint available.

tickler file US term for a collection of memorandums filed in chronological order to remind somebody to do certain tasks as scheduled.

tied outlet Retail outlet that is financially backed by a manufacturer on condition that the outlet sells the manufacturer's goods. Most public houses in the UK, for example, are tied outlets.

tie-up Arrangement whereby a large company helps to finance a smaller company, thus gaining rights in some or all of its developments. Tie-ups most often occur where the receiving company is developing in high-technology areas.

till money Banknotes and coins held by a bank, known as vault money in the USA.

time-adjusted rate of return Alternative term for ***internal rate of return***.

time and motion Study of the way in which a particular job is carried out, in an effort to streamline the physical actions involved and so save time.

time card Alternative term for ***clock card***.

time cost Alternative term for ***period cost***.

time deposit Cash deposited in a bank and earning interest (as opposed to a non-interest earning demand deposit).

time of supply Alternative term for ***tax point***.

time preference Theory of interest which suggest that interest is the price paid by a borrower for immediate consumption, and compensation to the lender, who loses the opportunity to use the articles or money lent for his or her own purposes. Therefore, time preference is a person's preference for current rather than future consumption, or *vice versa*.

time rate Payment for work done on the basis of how long the job takes. *See also* ***piece rate***.

time-series analysis Analysis of a company's financial statements over several periods of time. *See also* ***cross-section analysis***.

time sheet Document that records the time a worker or machine spends on each activity in a particular period, used mainly for costing purposes.

time value of money Theory which postulates that one's money is more valuable now than at any time in the future, whether it be in a hour's time, next week or next year. For example, the earlier money is received the sooner it can be invested to earn interest, and the later it is paid out the longer it will earn interest.

timing difference Alternative term for ***temporary difference***.

TIN Abbreviation of ***taxpayer identification number***.

tip Cash given to somebody who has rendered a service, over and above the payment agreed. It is also known as a gratuity.

top-up loan Alternative term for ***margin loan***.

total assets Total of all of a company's assets (as opposed to net assets).

total assets turnover Turnover calculated as sales divided by total assets.

total cost of production Alternative term for ***production cost***.

total costs Total of all expenditure incurred in an accounting period, often divided into fixed costs and variable costs.

total income Taxpayer's income from all sources, used in calculating income tax.

total production cost of finished goods Alternative term for ***manufacturing cost of finished goods***.

total profits Company profits that are charged to corporation tax.

total standard cost Sum of the standard cost allowance for non-production overhead and the total standard production cost.

total standard production cost Sum of the standard fixed overhead cost, standard variable overhead cost, standard direct labour cost and standard direct materials cost.

total standard profit Sales at standard selling price less standard overhead cost of sales.

TPI Abbreviation of ***tax and price index***.

trade acceptance Document prepared by a seller that is signed (accepted) by the buyer when goods or services are purchased. It is then a note payable of the buyer and a note receivable of the seller.

trade credit Credit one company or business gives to another, usually in the form of time to pay for goods and services supplied.

trade creditor Company or person to whom money is owed as a result of normal trading. *See* ***accounts payable***.

trade debtor Company or person who owes money as a result of normal trading. *See* ***accounts receivable***.

trade discount Discount on list price offered to trade customers, i.e., to customers likely to place large and regular orders. It recognizes the value of the customer concerned.

trade-in Acquisition of an asset in exchange for an existing one, possible with some additional money.

trademark Logo or name (a trade name), often labelled TM, used to distinguish one manufacturer's product from another's. Registered trademarks may not be used by another manufacturer in the country of registration.

trade payables Payables that arise in the normal course of trading (which includes most accounts payable).

trade receivables Receivables that arise in the normal course of trading (which includes most accounts receivable).

trade references List of trading partners to whom a company may refer if it wishes to confirm the creditworthiness of a potential customer.

trade secret Business or technical information kept by a company as a secret and therefore not generally known to competitors. If purchased it becomes an intangible asset.

trade terms Special conditions (usually discount prices) available to people working in the same industry or trade. *See **trade discount**.*

trading account First section of a profit and loss account, in which income and expenditure concerned in a company's trading activities are detailed. The final figure on this account is the company's gross profit.

trading on the equity US description of a company that engages in ***debt financing***.

trading loss Loss incurred while taking a principal (trading) position in a market. The loss must be recorded in the profit and loss account of a company. For this reason it is often disguised, where possible, by such tactics as 'redefining' it as a fixed asset investment or including it as an extraordinary below-the-line item in the accounts.

trading profit Profit a company makes before deductions of auditors' remuneration, directors' fees, and so on.

trading stamps Discount given by a retailer to its customers in the form of stamps. The stamps have a redemption value (in cash or goods) and the discount is represented by this value.

traditional costing Alternative US term for ***adsorption costing***.

tranche Slice or portion; an instalment. In general, one of a series of payments which when put together add up to the total agreed.

tranche funding Funding by making available to a new company successive sums of money (tranches), often conditional on the attainment of targets in its business plan.

transaction Internal or external event that affects the finances or operation of a business, resulting in an accounting entry. Sales and purchases are examples of external transactions; depreciation of an asset is an internal transaction.

transaction costs Costs incurred by certain transactions, such as sales and purchases.

transaction file Computer file in which internal or external transactions are recorded.

transfer of a going concern Under regulations for value added tax (VAT), the selling of a business owned by a VAT-registered trader to another registered trader does not attract VAT, i.e., there is no input tax for the buyer and no output tax for the seller.

transfer payment Payment made by the UK government that is not in return for goods or services, such as state pensions and unemployment benefit.

transfer price Within a group of companies, the price at which goods or services are sold by one subsidiary to another.

transferred-in costs In process costing, costs incurred by a department that are picked up by another department that succeeds it.

translation exposure Alternative term for ***accounting exposure***.

travel allowance Amount added to a person's salary to cover the cost of travelling to work, or for journeys undertaken in the course of work.

treasurer Person whose job is to look after a company's money and other assets.

treasury Government department that deals with national finance and government funding, and is responsible for the execution of the government's economic policy. Some large companies also have treasury departments.

trend analysis Use of ***accounting ratios*** to analyse the performance of a company over a given period.

trial balance Listing of all of a company's account balances. Credit balances are listed in one column and debit balances in another, and if the double-entry book-keeping has been accurate the totals of each column will be the same. After adjustment, if necessary, the trial balance figures are used to draw up the profit and loss account and the balance sheet. *See also* ***unadjusted trial balance***.

trickle-down theory Theory that money put into the pockets of those who are already rich through government policy is thought to seep down into the hands of those who are less well off. Trickle-down is though to be a more effective way of redistributing wealth than transfer payments.

true and fair View of a company's affairs that an auditor of its accounts is required to take in giving an opinion.

Trueblood Report Report published in 1971 by the American Institute of Certified Public Accountants. It was prepared by a committee under the chairmanship of Robert Trueblood and called *Objectives of Financial Statements*. It identified that the making of economic decisions requires information provided by financial statements, and that this should be their basic objective.

turnover Gross value of all sales made by a company during an accounting period; total sales revenue. The term is also used for the rate at which stock or some other asset is turned over.

turnover ratio Accounting ratio that indicates the nubmer of times a circulating asset has been replaced within a given financial period.

two-column cash book Cash book that details receipts and payments but does not list discounts (allowed or received). *See also* ***three-column cash book***.

U

UITF Abbreviation of ***Urgent Issues Task Force***.

unabsorbed cost Production cost may be allocated to each unit produced over a specified level of output and represented as a percentage of that unit's overall cost to the producer. If the specified level of output is not reached, then some of the cost is not paid for, and is known as the unabsorbed cost.

unadjusted rate of return Alternative term for ***accounting rate of return***.

unadjusted trial balance Trial balance before any adjustments are made and any closing entries made at the end of the accounting period. *See* ***trial balance***.

unappropriated profits Part of a company's profits not distributed as dividends or set aside for a particular use.

unappropriated retained earnings Alternative term for ***unappropriated profits***.

unavoidable cost Cost that has to be met no matter what course of action is taken. *See also* ***avoidable cost***.

unbilled revenue Revenue earned in a particular accounting period but for which no invoices have been sent to customers.

uncertainty Event whose outcome can only be estimated, as opposed to ***risk***.

uncollectable account Account receivable that the debtor will not pay; a ***bad debt***.

unconsolidated subsidiary Subsidiary whose financial data is not included in the group's consolidated accounts.

uncontrollable cost Cost (fixed or variable) that management cannot directly control, either in the short or long term. *See also* ***controllable cost***.

underabsorbed overhead Also termed underapplied overhead, a situation in absorption costing in which the overhead costs actually incurred for a period are more than the absorbed overhead. It is a debit balance on the overhead account, resulting in a lower profit.

underapplied overhead Alternative term for ***underabsorbed overhead***.

undercapitalization Situation of a new company that does not have enough capital to take it through the initial burn-out period immediately after start-up. *See* ***burn rate***.

underground economy That part of an economy controlled by organized crime. It is better controlled and more concentrated than the ***black economy***.

underlying document Any record – invoice, receipt, voucher – that gives rise to an entry in a journal.

undistributable reserves Company reserves that may not be disrtibuted (as dividend to shareholders), including the capital redemption reserve, most unrealized profits, share capital and the share premium account.

undistributed earnings Alternative term for ***retained income***.

undistributed profit Company profit that has not been distributed as dividend to shareholders.

unearned income Income not derived from work or fees of office (such as divdends on shares and interest on investments). It is liable for income tax in the UK, at the same rate as earned income. In the USA, the term denotes advances received from customers (i.e., money received before goods or services are delivered), also called deferred credit or unearned revenue.

unearned revenue *See* ***unearned income***.

unemployment benefit Commonly known as the dole, a payment made in the UK by the State to somebody who is out of work and has previously paid a certain number of national insurance contributions.

unexpired cost Balance of company expenditure not written off to the profit and loss account, sometimes used in the USA to denote an asset that appears on the balance sheet. For example, the unexpired cost of an asset is its net book value.

unfavourable variance In standard costing, the amount by which the actual cost of a product exceeds the standard cost assigned to it. It is also called adverse variance.

unfunded Describing an existing liability for which no funds have yet been allocated.

unit Single item of production (*see* ***unit cost***), or a single area in a factory or shop, or a share in an investment.

unit cost Cost of producing one item. It is calculated by taking the total cost of production and dividing it by the number of units produced. It is used mainly in determining the price that should be charged for a product. A unit cost may also be assigned to sales (as the cost of selling one item).

unit price Price paid per unit bought or price charged per unit sold.

units of production method of depreciation Alternative term for ***production method of depreciation***.

unit standard operating profit Standard operating profit expressed per unit of production (or sales).

unit standard production cost Standard production cost expressed per unit of production (or sales).

unit standard selling price Standard selling price expressed per unit sold.

universal agent Agent with unlimited authority to close contracts on behalf of the principal. *See also* ***special agent***.

unlimited company Company that consists of members who are all liable for the total of the company's debts. *See* ***limited company***.

unlimited liability Liability of the members of an unlimited company, or of the general partners in a partnership, or of the sole proprietor of a sole proprietorship. *See* ***limited liability***.

unqualified opinion *See* ***auditor's opinion***.

unrealized gross margin In the instalment method of recognizing revenue, the profit that will eventually result when receivables have been collected.

unrealized profit Profit that results from holding assets (rather than employing them); profit not yet realized as cash.

unrealized loss Loss that results from holding assets (rather than employing them); loss not yet realized in cash terms.

unrecovered cost Asset's book value.

unsecured creditor Person who has made a loan but received no ***security***.

upstream Describing the movement of funds from a subsidiary company to its parent company.

Urgent Issues Task Force (UITF) Organization established in 1991 by the Accounting Standards Board to deal with urgent matters not already the subject of a standard.

usage rate Rate at which a raw material or other commodity is used up.

usage variance Alternative term for ***direct materials usage variance***.

usance Rate of interest on a loan, or ***unearned income*** derived from the ownership of wealth or capital.

useful economic life Time for which an asset provides economic benefit to its owner; the service life.

use of funds Any transaction that reduces a company's funds.

useful life *See* ***useful economic life***.

usury Moneylending at an excessive rate of interest, not in itself illegal.

V

valuation account Contra account that details a fall in market value of stock below cost. It enables valuations to be made on a ***lower of cost and market*** basis.

value Term that is not as precise as it may seem. The value of something is the price a buyer is prepared to pay for it, but this can fluctuate according to all sorts of variables, for example whether it is a buyer's market or a seller's market, to what use the buyer will be putting the item, and so on. Usually the term is qualified, to minimize possible confusion.

value added Difference between the price a company or industry pays for its materials and the price at which it sells finished goods. For example, a used-car dealer may acquire a car, recondition the engine and repaint the body. When the dealer sells the car, the added value is the value of these operations as reflected in the new (higher) selling price of the car.

value-added statement Alternative term for ***added-value statement***.

value added tax (VAT) Form of indirect taxation in which the producer, seller and consumer pay a percentage of the value added to the product or service. For example, if a manufacturer buys raw materials at £10 per unit and sells each unit of product for £20, the value added is £10. The manufacturer is required to pay a percentage of the £20 in VAT, and can claim back the VAT paid on the £10-worth of materials. VAT in the UK is 17.5 per cent for most things (since April 1991), although some goods and services are exempt and some zero-rated.

value for money audit Audit of a non-profit making organization, such as a charity or government department, to check that it working efficiently and giving value for money.

value in exchange Value of something as form of exchange, rather than as an object of use. For example, precious stones are worth virtually nothing in terms of real value in use but because they are rare and desirable, they command a high price. *See also* ***value in use***.

value in use Value of something to the person using it, which may be different to the sale value of the object. For example, a machine may be valuable to its owner because it produces goods for sale, whereas it may be valueless in itself, perhaps because it cannot be moved. In accounting terms, an asset's value in use can be calculated by discounting the future cash flows that would accrue from its continued use. *See also* ***value in exchange***.

value to the business For an asset, the replacement cost or the recoverable amount (higher of net present value and net realizable value), whichever is the lower.

value variance Alternative term for ***price variance***.

variable budget Alternative term for ***flexible budget***.

variable cost Also called direct cost, an expense that varies with the level of activity, such as costs incurred in production that vary depending on the quantity of output. *See also* ***semi-variable costs***.

variable costing Alternative term for ***direct costing***.

variable cost percentage Variable cost ratio expressed as a percentage.

variable cost ratio Also called variable expense ratio, the ratio of all variable costs to sales revenue.

variable expense ratio Alternative term for ***variable cost ratio***.

variable overhead cost Part of a product's indirect costs that vary in proportion to the quantity produced or sold. Consumable materials and salesperson's commission are examples of variable overhead cost.

variable production overhead Part of a product's indirect manufacturing costs that vary in proportion to the quantity produced or sold. Depreciation of machinery and amount of power consumed are examples of a variable production overhead.

variable-rate mortgage Mortgage whose rate of interest may be varied by the mortgagee to suit conditions on the money market.

variance In standard costing, the difference between actual results obtained and those budgeted for or expected. If the former is larger than the latter, it is a favourable variance; if the latter is greater than the former, it is an unfavourable variance.

variation analysis In standard costing, the examination of variances to determine why they occurred.

VAT Abbreviation of ***value added tax***.

VATman Colloquial term for a Customs and Excise employee who deals with ***value added tax*** (VAT)

vault money US term for ***till money***.

vendor Person who sells goods or services.

venture capital Also known as risk capital, capital invested in a venture (usually a young company, often in high-technology areas) that presents a risk.

verifiability Ability to check the accuracy of a financial statement by tracing documentary evidence that gave rise to an entry.

verification Method used by an auditor to check the accuracy of a financial statement by, for example, tracing documentary evidence that gave rise to an entry. The auditor may also seek ***confirmation*** from outside sources.

vertical form Method of arranging a financial statement with debits and credits one above the other (as opposed to horizontal form).

vertical diversification Diversification into industries or businesses at different stages of production. *See also* ***horizontal diversification***.

vertical integration Amalgamation of companies involved in different stages of production in the same industry, for example to form one company capable of extracting raw materials, using them to produce goods and then distributing and selling the manufactured product.

vested interest Reason (e.g., an investment) or possible benefit that a person may have for maintaining a certain state of affairs.

view to resale Reason for excluding a subsidiary company's figures from the consolidated accounts of a group (because the subsidiary was acquired specifically for selling on).

virement Method of allowing an overspend on one part of a budget to be offset by an underspend on another part. Not all systems of budgetary control allow this practice.

visible Describing something that can be seen, identified or counted, such as visible assets (more usually called tangible assets).

volume Number of units traded (as opposed to turnover, which is the value of the units traded, although the terms are sometimes interchanged).

volume variance In standard costing, the difference between the absorbed fixed overhead and the amount budgeted for.

voluntary liquidation Also termed voluntary winding-up, the liquidation of a company that has decided to cease trading, rather than one that has gone bankrupt.

voucher Document (such as a receipt or invoice) that supports or proves entries in a book of prime entry. A voucher is also the name given to a paper given in place of money (such as a gift voucher or a luncheon voucher).

voucher system System of controlling cash, common in the USA, in which every company cheque has to authorized by an approved voucher. Only petty cash can be used as a source of actual cash.

vouching In auditing, a substantive test to check that a company's records correctly identify the type of transactions entered into.

W

WACC Abbreviation of ***weighted average costs of capital***.

wage Payment made to a worker, normally at a fixed rate per hour, day or week (and usually paid weekly). *See also* ***piece rate***.

wage differential Difference between levels of wages, caused by many variables, such as occupation, industry, sex and age of employee, geographical location, experience and qualification of the employee, and so on.

wage freeze Situation in which wages are fixed for a certain period of time, either by government authority on a national level or by agreement within a single company or industry.

wage-price spiral Form of inflation. If a producer is forced to increase wages, he or she must increase the price of the product to cover the increased wages cost, which in turn leads to new wage demands by workers.

wages costs Alternative term for ***labour costs***.

wages oncost *See* ***oncost***.

waiting time Time an employee spends not working, i.e., waiting for a machine to warm up or be repaired, or waiting for another employee to finish the previous stage of a job.

walk-through test Method of evaluating an accounting system. Some transactions are selected from the records and followed through each stage of the system.

warranty Promise by a manufacturer or seller to correct any defects in goods sold. In some manufacturing companies, an amount is estimated as possible warranty expense and treated as a liability.

waste *See* ***spoilage***.

wasting asset Asset that has a limited useful life (such as a natural resource that becomes depleted as it is consumed).

waybill *See* ***consignment note***.

WDA Abbreviation of ***writing-down allowance***.

WDV Abbreviation of ***written-down value***.

wealth tax Tax levied annually on wealth (which is notoriously difficult to define). It is used in some European countries but not in the UK.

wear and tear Popular and legal term for ***depreciation***. It is the decrease in value of an item due to deterioration through normal use rather than through accident or negligence.

weighted-average cost *See* ***average cost***.

weighted average cost of capital (WACC) Way of determining a company's cost of capital by assigning a required rate of return to each source of funds on its balance sheet. The size of the source is then used to weight the required return and the WACC expressed as a percentage by dividing the total return by the total weights.

wholesaler Person who buys goods in bulk from a producer and then sells them in smaller quantities to retailers or other wholesalers, earning a profit either by charging a commission to the retailer or by adding to the manufacturer's price. *See* ***markup***.

wholly-owned subsidiary Subsidiary whose shares are all owned by the parent company.

windfall gains and losses Gain or loss resulting from circumstances outside the control of the recipient (such as changes in the net present value of earnings because of changes in discount rates).

winding-up Cessation of a company's business activity and the start-up of its liquidation.

window dressing Alternative term for ***creative accounting***.

WIP Abbreviation of ***work in progress***.

withdrawals Assets distributed to the owner, usually in a partnership. *See* ***partner's drawing***.

withholding Deduction from wages or salary, made by an employer usually to pay income tax, which the employer remits to the tax authority.

withholding tax Tax on the interest on a deposit or investment deducted at source (the depositor or investor receives net interest).

with the exception of *See* ***except for***.

working assets All the assets of a company except its ***capital assets***; current assets less current liabilities. They include outstanding debts, stocks of raw materials, work in progress, stocks of finished goods and cash in hand.

working capital Capital available for the day-to-day running of a company, used to pay such expenses as salaries, purchases, and so on.

working-capital cycle Alternative term for ***operating cycle***.

working capital provided by operations Company revenue less operating expenses that use working capital.

working-capital ratio Alternative term for ***current assets ratio***.

working papers Documents prepared by an auditor in carrying out an audit, before issuing an opinion.

work in process Usual US term for ***work in progress***.

work in progress (WIP) Value of goods currently under manufacture or services being supplied, but not completed at the end of an accounting period. When entered into an account it is valued at cost or net realizable value, whichever is the lower.

work sheet *See **spreadsheet***.

worst moment concept In preparing financial projections and budgets, a concept that takes into account the worst times in a cash flow (such as periods when bills have to be paid) as well as the easier times.

worth Value. *See also **net worth***.

worth-debt ratio Inverse of the ***debt-equity ratio***.

write down To take the cost of an asset and deduct the amount by which it has depreciated in capital terms. This gives its written-down or book value. *See also **depreciation***.

write off To charge the whole of the value of an asset to expenses or loss (i.e., assign it zero value on the balance sheet). It is also known as charge off in the USA. ***Bad debts*** may also be written off.

write up To increase the value of an asset without recording any spend on it (i.e., there is no corresponding transaction).

writing-down allowance (WDA) Capital allowance in the UK for plant and machinery used in business. For industrial buildings, for example, it is 4% of initial cost; for company cars costing more than £12,000, it is limited to £3000 (25%).

written-down value (WDV) *See **write down***.

Y

yield Return on an investment, taking into account the annual income and the capital value of the investment, usually expressed as a percentage. There are also various other methods of calculating yield.

Z

zero-based budget (ZBB) Budget calculated as through it were being prepared for the first time using a zero base (with no initial commitment to spend on any activity).

zero-rated goods and services Goods and services that are liable for UK ***value added tax*** (VAT) but are currently rated at zero tax.

zero salvage value Under US tax regulations, a depreciable asset whose salvage value is estimated at less than 10% of its cost can be assigned a salvage value of zero.